Nathan Sheppard

Heroic Stature

Five addresses

Nathan Sheppard

Heroic Stature
Five addresses

ISBN/EAN: 9783337214227

Printed in Europe, USA, Canada, Australia, Japan

Cover: Foto ©ninafisch / pixelio.de

More available books at **www.hansebooks.com**

Heroic Stature

Five Addresses

By

Nathan Sheppard

Author of "Before an Audience," etc., etc.

Philadelphia
American Baptist Publication Society
MDCCCXCVII

PUBLISHERS' NOTE

THE matter of this book was found among Professor Sheppard's effects by his executors. On being examined by them and by the publishers' readers, these "Addresses" seemed to merit preservation by reason of their many qualities of excellence, presenting so much of inspiring thought and so fitting an exposition of the style of a man once prominent before the public.

All the immediate members of Professor Sheppard's family have gone with him into the world beyond. Most of those into whose hands this book will fall, have never met or seen him. There are a few who will recall the bright, pungent letters written by him for the "Examiner," over the pseudonym of "Keynote." Others, especially in England and Scotland, will

Publishers' Note

recall the various lectures which he delivered. To all of these, the publishers are sure, these addresses will come as a grateful remembrance of the one who was once with them. It will be a pleasant thought to some who hold Professor Sheppard's memory dear, that by this posthumous book his work shall still go forward.

The publishers have sought for a fitting dress for the book that thereby its reception may be more favorable and its circulation more wide. The book is believed by them to be in every way worthy of the attention of the Christian public.

CONTENTS

THE HUMAN MARTIN LUTHER . . . 1

JOHN WESLEY 59

NORMAN MACLEOD 109

CHARLES G. FINNEY 149

HUGH LATIMER 191

THE HUMAN MARTIN LUTHER

I

WE are to consider the great Protestant leader from a human point of view.

For three generations he was of German peasant stock; farther than that the biographers do not go.

Father, grandfather, and great-grandfather peasants! Where did Luther get his brains? Reversion doubtless—probably descended from a Viking king. Son of a peasant farmer, he says, it was not written in the stars that he was to become a doctor of divinity, or that he should pull the pope's hair and marry a runaway nun. But it was written in the stars that he was to do more for the emancipation of the human mind from ecclesiastical bondage than any other man.

Ancestry and Start

He sits high in all the people's hearts now, for Catholics and Jews joined in the fourth centennial celebration at Eisleben, where Martin Luther was born on the tenth of November, 1483, at eleven at night precisely.

At seven years of age he was sent to a free school; there was a free school in Germany four hundred years ago. He had five brothers, of whom we have never heard. It exhausted them to make him. Five-sixths of us go to the making of the one-sixth—who get all the offices. It must be uncomfortable to have one's only fame consist in a famous brother. The more distinguished he, the more extinguished you.

Two footsore and weary students arrived in Magdeburg with staff in hand, and on their backs knapsacks containing all their worldly goods. They had come to study at a famous school of the town. One of these boys was Martin Luther. He was fourteen years of age. They sang under the windows of the rich, and begged for bread and alms. It was called the "bread chorus." The windows of the rich have heard it many a time since, and may hear it many a time again before

Ancestry and Start

my esteemed contemporary, Mr. Arnold, and his remnant, put a stop to the worship of lubricity and duplicity, and set the world to rights.

He went from the school at Magdeburg to the school at Eisenach, where a wisehearted woman, Ursula Cotta by name, gave the boy Martin a home and met his four years' expenses. Nor did she offer to subscribe the trousers if some other woman would furnish all the arithmetics, according to the stratagem of him who subscribes on condition that the rest of us shall help him get the name and credit of it.

At eighteen years of age he was a student at the University of Erfurt, where his father was then able to support him until he secured his degree.

He dipped into theology, then into the law. He did not like the drudgery of the law, or the subtleties of theology. He was fond of rhetoric and oratory, poetry and music. He was rhetorical and oratorical from the beginning to the end of his career. He learned to play upon the guitar and flute, a good example to all

The Human Martin Luther

young parsons and other young men—pick up some source of amusement to which you can flee to escape the blues. It will help you; it may help others.

The human Martin Luther had a very human temper. The violence of his disposition was derived from both parents—not to mention his school teachers, one of whom we are told licked him fifteen times in one day for not knowing what he was never taught. If he had been a young American Protestant he would probably have thrashed the teacher. He says he often hid in the chimney corner until the storm of his dear father's wrath blew over. His mother too was inordinately addicted to the rod. Both of his parents were passionate and affectionate, and so was he. The most savage dispositions have intervals of extreme tenderness.

His Violent Temper

Luther's father's coat of arms was a hammer on a granite block, and that well typified what Luther afterward became—a hammer on a granite block.

His Sense of the Marvelous

Looking at him from a human point of view, we will make note of prominent characteristics. His sense of the marvelous was one. He was what we call superstitious from first to last—an indefinite word, but definite enough as applied to him. Necessarily superstitious from his being born and bred a Roman Catholic in 1483 instead of in 1883, when it is so easy for Monseigneur Capel to boast of how much range the reason is allowed by the pope. The range allowed to reason by the pope is the range of reason allowed by—reason.

A flash of lightning set Luther's sense of the marvelous on fire. He could not resist such a summons. He fell to the ground; it was the call of God to him, a call to the convent. He implored Saint Ann to help him to become a monk, and a monk he became. This is a striking illustration of the fact that a man's wish may be considered God's call, and that a strong predisposition may be confounded with an answer to a prayer.

The Human Martin Luther

He remained three years in the convent at Erfurt. He developed rapidly and enormously in a religious experience of the monastic type, morbid, malarial, a low malarial fever being mistaken for high spiritual fervor, in which vanity passed for humility, and self-indulgence for self-denial. For a man makes himself believe that in going through the observances he is crucifying himself, whereas he is really glorifying himself.

A Monastic Type of Piety

As the result of this type of piety Luther became the victim of a morbid self-examination. He accused himself as though he were guilty of crime, when he was guilty of only one crime, the crime of a false self-accusation. It is not impossible to hear now from the pulpit a prayer which would insure an indictment by the grand jury if the man were telling the truth. Thou shalt not bear false witness against thyself.

Victim of a Morbid Self-examination

No half-hearted monk was the boy Luther. He was a whole-hearted monk,

His First Turning=point

a monk of the monks was he. Monks pray; he prayed without ceasing. Monks fast; he fasted till you could see the ribs through his skin. Monks do penance; he did penance, flogging himself and starving himself, and confining himself in a dark cell, until he was found prostrate, emaciated, almost dead with his attempts to please God by disobeying his commandments. The severity of his early discipline had contributed to the unhealthful gloom that drove him into the convent.

In this convent, we are told, Luther read the whole of the Bible for the first time. Some assert that he was ignorant up to this time of Paul's Epistles. Are we to conclude that the Epistles did for Luther what the Gospels alone were not able to do? that Paul succeeded where Jesus failed? At all events he seems to have been indebted to Paul for a revolution in his religion. Paul and he were congenial. He was enamored of Paul's method of controversial statement, reveled in the very things hard to be understood, and made them no easier to be understood by explaining them.

He felt the necessity of a vocabulary that admits of pulmonary eloquence, like those who prefer the old version to the new, because it is easier for them to produce an effect with the word damnation, than with the thing condemnation. They would rather damn a man than condemn him, because they are under the impression that the man would prefer to be condemned. Paul's influence upon Luther would make a psychological-theological study of rare interest.

The precise meaning of his "justification by faith" has occasioned much discussion, into which we shall not enter. There is no doubt that the ferment of Luther's mind precluded exact thinking, and that it was something of a tangle to himself. When Dr. Jonas complained to him that he could not follow him in his sermons, Luther replied, "I cannot follow myself; I am too wordy."

But our topic is not so much Luther's doctrines as how he handled them and

His First Turning=point

himself. Ours is not a doctrinal but a personal; not a spiritual but a human point of view.

This change or revolution was emotional, rather than intellectual. With that understanding it is not necessary for him, or his biographers, or us to get a definite idea of what this change amounted to, so far as his theological opinions are concerned. He had a tumultuous experience in the convent. He was sometimes prostrate under a sense of unpardonable sin, and sometimes rose into a delirium of ecstasy from a sense of forgiveness. He rose out of his stupor with a devouring passion for making himself a better man, and his church a better church, and his world a better world. A temperament this, not for keeping the commandments, but for public speaking. It soon showed itself, and was soon recognized. From this time he was a great public speaker and agitator, for he had the oratorical temperament. He was nervous. No man can be too nervous for a public speaker, provided he keeps on the sane side of the line—if anybody can tell where that is.

Luther was quick-witted, passionate, combative, aggressive, droll, with an abundance of animal magnetism, and a large vocabulary by nature, and a quick, accurate, natural ear for the rhythm of rhetoric; in short, he was endowed and equipped for an outdoor leader—a leader of the people. He had neither the kind of courage, nor the balance, nor the judgment, nor the tact, required in a leader of thought or a teacher of ideas.

He had the courage that draws its nourishment from collision, its stimulation from opposition. His fire was like that of the flints, it needed friction to draw it out. Before the mob and before the pope, and before governors and kings, he was audacious and aggressive; in the quiet of his study he was hesitating and vacillating. This is temperament. The opinions he proclaimed in public with so much boldness, were spoken of with misgivings when he reflected upon them in private. He exclaimed:

Priest and Professor

"I never feel prouder, more full of lofty daring, than when I hear their denunciations. What care I for the whole mob of them, doctors, bishops, and princes."

But when the denunciation dies away then dies away the delirium it occasioned. Many a time the preacher imagines he has torn everybody to pieces, but finds that he has torn nobody to pieces but himself.

He was ordained as a priest at twenty-four, and became a professor of philosophy at the University of Wittenberg at twenty-five. Now watch him feel his way. Did you ever feel your way in the dark?

His lectures drew crowds of students and created a sensation. They were searching, sweeping, bold. The young priest was evidently feeling his way into a line of thought of his own. The thunder in him began to come out. Lecturing brought it out. Lecturing is the oldest of the forms of public instruction, and will hold its own with any and all of them to the end.

The audience was made up of professors,

students, nobles, princes, common people, and they were all amazed at his boldness, fascinated by his originality, startled by his heresies. Another heretic is rising. He will certainly make a stir, but what kind of a stir? He will certainly be a leader, but whither will he lead? What was the young man driving at?

His next great experience was a long journey. Traveling revolutionizes opinions, often uproots convictions; makes short work of long-entrenched ideas, early education, parental influence; changes character for good or evil.

Another Turning Point

As he approached the capital of Christendom, he thought of it with awe and looked upon it with reverence; he would nourish his faith with its memories and observances. He fell upon his knees, and exclaimed, "Hail, Holy Rome!" but he no sooner beheld it than he beheld its corruption. He had expected to find the highest faith, he really found the lowest form of unbelief, and disbelief, and misbelief. From the pope down the hierarchy was bad, bad, bad. The priests laughed at their own doctrines and rites. They carried around the consecrated wafer on a beautiful white stallion. He says, "A good Italian is as great a prodigy as a black swan."

He was next a doctor of divinity, lecturer at the university, and town preacher. It was a transition period. He felt his responsibility and shrank from it; he told his friends that they had put too much upon him. He shrank, but went forward; dreaded to speak, but spoke out. It was not for want of self-confidence that he shrank. He had self-confidence and self-depreciation both, a common combination in public speakers and leaders of men.

The most effective popular leaders are made up of these two contradictory elements warring in their members, an exterior self-assertion, and an interior awful sense of deficiency—a defiant front and the perspiration running down the back. He threw himself into his work with just that peculiar quality of zeal and pluck which comes of just such shrinking self-depreciation as his. Apprehension of failure is an element of success.

Leo X., pope of Rome, wanted money with which to finish St. Peter's, and instead of getting a mortgage, he sent the rascally monk, Tetzel, to Germany with indulgences for sale.

Another Turning Point Still

The last thought of the first Christians was a gorgeous house of worship, and the first thought of the last Christians is a gorgeous mortgaged house of worship, which echoes with—yes, that's the trouble—it is so constituted that you can hear nothing of the gospel but its echoes. Hence you never hear a church in the New Testament say one word about raising money to pay a debt, and you never hear anything in some churches of our day but an appeal for money, or else an appeal for some one to come and persuade them to give what they say they have not in their possession to give, cash.

Tetzel mounted his auction block and exclaimed:

The Ninety-five Propositions

"Is your friend or relative roasting in purgatory? The moment your money chinks in the pope's chest, that moment your friend's soul flies to heaven." "Saint Stephen gave himself up to be stoned and Saint Bartholomew to be skinned, now will you not at least make the sacrifice of a small donation to save your souls?"

This donation bought a letter of indulgence, which allowed the bearer to water the stock of the company, or freeze out the other stockholders, or confiscate any man's property that stood in his way, provided he was in his pew every Sunday morning, with a long face and a loud voice. A pew may be as much of a self-indulgence as an opera box. Are we quite sure that an auction sale of pews is not a sale of indulgences?

Luther's students went to hear Tetzel and told Luther what Tetzel said. Students love a row. They found Luther in just the state of inflammability adequate for their purpose. Behold how great a forest a little fire kindleth.

The Human Martin Luther

He was now twenty-eight years of age. He was young, but he had learned how to handle himself before an audience. All his qualities and qualifications came into play—even his very defects were aids. His violent temper roused the German phlegm. He was in his element—controversy, hand to hand, out-door, pugnacious polemics. He was young, roused, and mad. The angry spot doth glow on Cæsar's brow.

No other kind of man was equipped for such a work as this—no mere scholar, or theologian, or fastidious critic, or purist in rhetoric; no Melancthon, or Erasmus, or Calvin. The human Martin Luther was needed for the human Martin Luther's work.

He attacked Tetzel with all the vehemence, and with all the indefiniteness and ambiguity, of his nature. A young lion roared against him and he rent him as he would a kid, with a very indefinite idea of what the lion was talking about. He challenged Tetzel and all the rest of them to a discussion, according to custom, by

The Ninety-five Propositions

writing out and nailing up ninety-five propositions, or theses, upon the pillars of the church of All Saints. That was October 31, 1517. This country had been discovered only twenty-five years.

It is sufficient for our purpose here to quote but some portions of these propositions:

No. 1. "When Christ commands us to repent he intends that our whole life shall be one of repentance."

No. 7. "God forgives the sins of no one who is not willing to obey his confessor."

No. 32. "Those who think themselves sure of salvation by indulgences will go to perdition with those who taught them so."

No. 71. "Cursed be he who speaks against the indulgence of the pope."

No. 72. "But blessed be he who speaks against the foolish and impudent language of the preachers of indulgences."

No. 86. "'Why,' ask the common people, 'does not the pope, who is richer than Crœsus, build St. Peter's with his own money instead of that of poor Christians?'"

(Perhaps because rich men often make poor Christians. They do not give lest they should prevent those from giving who have nothing to give. So nobody gets anything until somebody dies, and then the lawyers get it.)

These propositions may sound tame to us, but they were bold for him and his circumstances; nor do they dovetail any better than some of the planks of our wonderful party platforms; but that itself is illustrative of Luther's intellect, position, and circumstances.

He was still feeling his way; he was always feeling his way. Who is not? He says himself, these ninety-five propositions "were advanced more by way of argument than in a positive manner." Speaking of what was called his "furious attack" in these theses, he says: "I did not know what indulgence was, and the tune was pitched too high for my voice."

But the voice rose to the tune, and the people rose to the voice. It was another voice crying in the wilderness, but it lacked the definiteness and explicitness of

John the Baptist's cry. Few reformers know so well what they are working for as John the Baptist did.

He could not look into the fields of time and say which grain would grow and which would not, but he could sow seeds with a free hand, and some of them have grown, or a Quaker boy would not be writing this.

We do not disparage him; we merely explain him. His method of action is beyond the reach of microscopic criticism, and we must give the leviathan room to disport himself. Mr. Matthew Arnold calls him a "Philistine of genius, who had a coarseness and lack of spiritual delicacy which has harmed his disciples."

He certainly was no æsthete. If he had come to this country he would have come in the "Mayflower," and not in the "Sunflower." I came over in the "William Penn" and am another Philistine, and a Quaker Philistine at that; hence the anti-ecclesiastical bias of this discourse.

Yes, coarse he was perhaps, coarse like the plow that has roots to tear up, coarse like the bulldog that has a bull to throw. And the bulldog threw the bull. Headlong, headstrong, but heartright and upright was this man Luther.

Luther was now at bay. A brave man at bay is a scene to admire, and men glory in him. Martin Luther at bay is a historical scene. It was an event, and was destined to change events. It brought his great cause to a great crisis. Feeling his way until he found himself at bay, he was forced to go farther than he would have gone, and compelled to take a position that he never would have taken. The attempt and not the deed confounded him.

Luther at Bay

He did not intend to secede from the Romish Church; he intended to stay in it and reconstruct it, but it was not so to be. Events are often too much for the men who create them. The Reformation was now leading the Reformer, instead of the Reformer the Reformation.

The pope might have won him by conciliatory tact, but he preferred the course which Protestantism would have chosen,

No Retreat

the coercion which would bring on a collision, which in turn would ensure victory to Luther. The pope excommunicated Luther, and thus Leo X. created the first great Protestant Reformer.

Then there was a stir and a commotion. The pope's Bull of excommunication arrived in Germany, and the students took it from the bookseller's shop and tore it to pieces. Luther burned it at the gates of the town amid acclamations and exultations. Tetzel had burned Luther's ninety-five propositions, Luther burned the pope's anathema.

Luther once at issue with the whole power of Rome there was no retreat. He must go forward. Confused motives within him and confused noises around him, there he stood, bewildered but unabashed. He had groped his way to a point from which he dared not, could not, recede. He had set out to make a better man of himself, a better church of his church, and a better world of his world. But his church repudiated him, and the world was divided

The Human Martin Luther

on account of him. He went out to war before he heard the "moving in the tops of the mulberry trees," but now he must fight on.

Just here we, from our point of view in time and circumstances, can see distinctly a profound principle disentangle itself from the confused noises:

No religious authority can be accepted without religion; destitute of religion the man is destitute of authority, whatever may be his costume or credentials.

There is not a more dramatic scene in all history, or a more picturesque figure, than Luther arraigned before the diet at Worms.

Before the Diet at Worms

He left Wittenberg in a carriage surrounded by his friends from the university and the town, who filled the air with shouts and prayers and benedictions. "Do not desert us," they cried. The villages welcomed him as he passed. They drank his health at the hotels, and cheered him with merry music. A priest sent him a portrait of Savonarola, and urged him to be manful for the truth. At

Before the Diet at Worms

Weimar they were posting an edict requiring all who had Luther's books to give them up. He was asked if this sign deterred him, and he replied, "I will go on if they kindle a fire between Wittenberg and Worms that reaches heaven."

His health succumbed to the excitement, and his spirits failed with his failing strength. The spirits of the bravest depend upon the brave man's health; words will not do.

In spite of bad health and low spirits he held a public discussion at Heidelberg, and pushed on. As he approached the imperial city and its dread ordeal, his friends weakened and sought to deter him. But he answered:

"I am resolved to enter Worms, although as many devils should set at me as there are tiles on the housetops."

And he did enter Worms, and enter the diet, and stand in the presence of all the pomp and power of Germany and of Rome, civil and ecclesiastical. The emperor of Germany, Charles V., sat upon a throne high and lifted up, clad in the royal purple.

Below him in the chair of State sat his brother Frederick. Before him was the pope's nuncio, clothed in full canonicals, and holding in his hand the thunders of the Vatican, which at that day made monarchs tremble and held nations in subjection. Grouped around were the princes and great officers of Church and State; knights and nobles in their yellow cloaks, the representatives of the free cities in black, the bishops in violet, the cardinals in blazing scarlet, the chivalry of Germany in their coats of mail and with glittering swords.

Everything and everybody, in short, was so disposed and arranged as to dazzle the imagination, confound the understanding, and overwhelm the judgment. Luther was ushered into the presence of this transcendent array of learning, power, authority, and impudence—ecclesiastical impudence, which transcends every other kind of impudence of which we have any knowledge or conception.

He was only thirty-eight years of age, and was not the Luther of later days,

Before the Diet at Worms

obese and hearty. He weighed only about one hundred and fifty pounds. He was emaciated and pallid; he had come from hard study, and was still ill; his body was consumed with disease, his mind with apprehension. He felt awfully alone. As he approached the imperial presence an old warrior greeted him with the remark: "My good monk, you are going a path such as I and our captains, in our hardest fight, have never trodden."

He showed signs of bewilderment. His voice was feeble, contrasting with the voice of the awful power that called him to account. This is what makes him human to us and fascinating, incomparably fascinating. Glorious human Martin Luther!

He was asked if he acknowledged the books before him as his. He answered in a low tone and a tone of alarm, "Yes." Will he recant them? He hesitated, and there was a dead silence. He asked for a day in which to frame an answer, and it was granted.

The council adjourned. Every man of

it probably believed that the monk was going to retract. What else could he mean by delay?

It was a crisis in the history of the great Reformation. The second day came. The august diet reassembled, and again Luther was asked if he will retract. He replied at length, in a dignified and astute argument, for he had prepared himself well. He asked for a discriminating judgment of his books. They differed widely; surely they could not all be equally obnoxious.

But the council was not there for consultation with him, but for judgment upon him. They demanded a direct answer to their question, will he recant?

Then came the memorable, imperishable words:

"Since your imperial majesty demands a direct answer, I will give you one that has neither horns nor teeth. Except I be convinced by Scripture and reason, I neither can, nor dare, retract anything. My conscience is a captive to God's word, and it is neither safe nor right to go against conscience."

At this point, according to some reports, there was a tremendous confusion, in which Luther was taunted by ecclesiastics, and finally ended by the exclamation, "Here I take my stand; I can do no otherwise. So help me God. Amen."

The council broke up, and that was the breaking up of the Roman Catholic power in Germany. The beginning of the end had come. The Reformation was to go forward; Germany was lost to the pope forever, Scotland soon was to be, and England. The United States, a new nation that was yet to be, was never to come under the Roman, nor any other ecclesiastical domination.

The human Martin Luther's fight with the pope involved a fight with the human Martin Luther. He had his conscience to fight as well as the vicegerent of the Almighty at St. Peter's. What a vicegerent. What a pope that conscience was. A wrong conscience upbraids with as much severity as a right one. It was no easier to make a better man of himself than to make a better church of his church.

It is much easier to advocate civil service reform than to practise it on yourself, if you are a candidate for the presidency. He says: "I feel how difficult it is to lay aside the scruples which I have had so long." "Oh, how much pain it has cost me to justify myself in standing alone against the pope. How many times have I asked myself what my enemies have asked me, Art thou alone wise? Can everybody else be mistaken?"

He says his suffering, his utter despair, cannot be conceived by others. He would sometimes wish to pass a sponge over what he had written.

One dramatic scene quickly followed another in the stirring drama of the Reformer's life. He disappeared from the publicity of the diet at Worms, and reappeared in the obscurity of the castle of Wartburg. On his way home from Worms he was spirited away to this remote and secluded castle by his friends to save his life.

In the Castle of Wartburg

In the Castle of Wartburg

Here he spent about a year in the disguise of a knight, hunting, writing, studying, translating the Bible, or meditating ways and means for circumventing the pope and promoting the Reformation.

He was hard at work on his translation of the Psalms in the lonely castle far away in the forest, shut out from the world, cut off from his followers. The singing of the birds and the sighing of the winds were the only sounds that reached him. Loneliness is a malady to so stormy a spirit as the human Martin Luther.

He was worn out with hard study and long fasting, and had had little sleep or recreation. He had forced his brain with whip and spur. He was afflicted with the disorders of body and mind, brought on by repeated violations of God's good laws. Finally the outraged imagination took revenge upon the will and overpowered it, and there rose before the miserable hermit, a spectre such as those that haunt the sleep of the diseased, the maniac, or the criminal. Alas, that religion should have to suffer for the indigestion of its teachers!

For Luther there was but one solution of the apparition: it was the devil. For Luther there was but one way of getting rid of him, to fight. He must take the aggressive. He seized his inkstand and hurled it at the spectre, and to this day they will show you where the Reformer's inkstand struck the—wall.

This was a very characteristic act, this throwing the inkstand at the devil. It opens out his nature to us, intellectual, psychological, theological, and illogical. It brings us to one of the forces that drove the marvelous piece of human machinery that we call the human Martin Luther, his belief in an evil being having almost as much power in the world as the Good Being who made it. He believed in the devil beyond even the age or his contemporaries. Some have been led by this to question his sanity. He certainly was unsane if not insane, as indeed any man is whose digestive apparatus upsets his thinking apparatus.

In the Castle of Wartburg

I have made up my mind that all these monster men were a little cracked, so if we are not very much cracked we may know that we are not very big men. Luther was sincere, at all events, and sincerity is one of the awful motive forces of the world.

He stopped eating and was found stretched insensible on the floor of his cell; that was the devil. He overworked his brain and lost his head; that was the devil. He over-excited his huge imagination until he had all the fantastic and preposterous visions of an opium eater, and that was the devil. He had the earache; that was the devil. He never had the neuralgia, or he would have thought two devils were fighting a duel on the inside of his head; or the rheumatism, or he would have thought he had a devil sawing at every joint.

He had a knife in his hand, and was half minded to cut his head off with it; that is the devil. The devil rattled the hazel nuts in the bag at night. If Luther had eaten them before going to bed the devil would have rattled them in the Reformer's stomach. He speaks of a man who tore off one of Satan's horns. Luther believed in this devil's miraculous power. He could smite with a malady that should slowly destroy life, or could suddenly arrest the course of a disease. He sent the storms, and the winds were his puffing and blowing.

He believed in demoniacal possession, that witchcraft was the devil's craft, that he could transform women into witches and send them riding through the air on broomsticks. He sometimes doubted the existence of God, but he never doubted the existence of the devil. Then again he was so beaten about that he did not know whether God was the devil or the devil was God. He encountered great devils who were learned doctors in theology, some of whom in the flesh are sometimes suspected of getting his Satanic majesty on the wrong throne.

He resorted to various devices for putting Satan to flight, a glass of wine, a strain on the violin, or a long prayer, and

One of the Lord's Anointed

always obliged the "old boy" to let go at last. All this seems pretty good evidence, including his glass of wine, that his devil was of his own creation and that when he put on his hat he put it on the—apparition at which he threw his inkstand. This was part of Luther's fight, this fight with the devil. He was contending with, not simply the pope, with his wide-spread, well-drilled army of cardinals, bishops, priests, and monks, but with these as the instruments of a malign deity who is disputing with a benign deity for supremacy in the world. Such was Luther's fight, a fight with the church, the flesh, and the devil.

Another motive force in the great Reformer was this: Martin Luther believed that Martin Luther was one of the Lord's anointed with all the prerogatives of one— just as the pope did and does. The kings of the earth set themselves, and the rulers take counsel together against the Lord and against his anointed.

He says, if he is restored to health he

will by God's help write against Erasmus and kill him. "He has insulted my Christ and must be punished." Also he says, "I killed Münzer, and his death at times weighed upon my conscience, but I killed him because he sought to kill my Christ."

The man has not been born who has the slightest shadow of authority for using such language or acting from such a motive. When his *saurkraut* disagreed with him, he charged it to the devil; when his associates disagreed with him, they disagreed with God.

And yet what an influence that motive has been in the history of the church. It has made the "Lord's anointed" a reproach and horror, from Luther to President Taylor of the Mormon hierarchy. The tap-root of Roman Catholicism is this assumption of police power in the name of the Deity, under the name and title of the Lord's anointed, and Luther carried it over into Protestantism, and there some of it remains to this day. Any man has it, whether he proclaims with Cromwell, "If God shall give you into my hands I will not spare a man of you," or with a Protestant preacher, that the Mormon religion should be put down by an army with rifles, and the infidel Turks driven out of the missionary's way with bayonets.

If Münzer, or the Mormons, or the Jews, or the atheists, or the agnostics, or the "peculiar people," break the law against disorder, vice, or crime, they are to be arraigned and punished by the civil authority, but there is no ecclesiastical tribunal that has authority over them except such as they voluntarily consent to obey.

The Christian has no ecclesiastical jurisdiction over the infidel, or the theist over the atheist, or the Gentile over the Jew, or the Protestant over the Catholic, or the Catholic over the Protestant, or the Protestant who keeps the new Sunday over the Protestant who keeps the old Sabbath.

He broke his vow and married a nun. Every old bachelor does that, especially if by so doing he can find another opportunity for playing the part of the Lord's anointed, who are no more to be desired as head of a house than as head of the State or the Church.

He said: "If I were to marry again I would carve an obedient wife for myself out of a block of marble, for unless I did I should despair of finding one."

Still, like all men of impulses, the impulse of tenderness was among the rest. The hardest men have soft spots, if not in their hearts, in their heads. He was never cross except when he was crossed. It was beautiful in him to send a letter of sympathy to Tetzel when he was dying of a broken heart in the cloister.

He was fond of fun, and full of it, after he had shaken off his monasticism and taken on some flesh. He that putteth his trust in the Lord shall be made fat. He said he would like to give the worms a good fat doctor to feed upon. He abandoned emaciation as a means of grace, and the sour monk became a jolly father. He relished nonsense and merry music and frolic, that would have broken the heart of good President Finney, who died deploring the rise and progress of croquet.

His Poverty

Luther's poverty is a farcical act in the tragedy of his career. After he was married and had a family and a home and was more than half-way through his great work and past the hardest of it, when he had the masses of Germany and many of its nobles and princes in his following, he was harassed by poverty and hectored with debt. Think of it! Protestantism was rich; Luther was poor. It is rich today and many of its preachers are starving.

"I am becoming more and more overwhelmed with debt. I shall be compelled to solicit alms by and by." "I have been obliged to pawn three goblets and sell one." Think of the leader of the Reformation reduced to such straits!

His strength was hunger-bitten. He was a dependent upon the Elector of Saxony, whose remittances were becoming suspiciously small and infrequent. Poverty is a fatality. It pursues some and nags them clean out of the world. It follows others like a ridiculous caprice.

There came still another turning-point. This time it was a turning-point for Christendom; Protestantism was organized. In 1529 we come upon the word Protestant. An imperial diet was assembled at Spires to take account of Luther's movement and put a stop to it. It decreed that the pope's Bull against Luther must be sustained and Luther silenced. The Lutherans present, made up of princes and dukes and a large following of the highest respectability, protested. The first Protestants were German princes.

Another Turning-Point

Then we have the Protestants in council at Augsburg, in 1530, where and when their first Confession of Faith was adopted. Protestantism was sown in power and raised in power. The movement now degenerated into a vituperative wrangle. Learning and ignorance, prelates high and low, poured out upon Luther an incessant torrent of malevolent abuse; but Luther was more than a match for them in the weapons of their choice.

He could return worse than he received;

Another Turning-point

he had a genius for invective, and was copiously endowed with the vocabulary of abuse. He delighted in the desolating wrath of words.

He denounced the followers who disagreed with him with no less acrimony than the enemies who opposed him outright. Erasmus broke with him in doctrine, and got the better of him in argument, whereupon Luther called him "a viper, a bug, a serpent, a fox, a knave, and an amphibolous being," reminding us of O'Connell calling the old Irish woman "the hypotenuse of a right-angled triangle."

The anger that sustained him in an open fight with words failed him in the arena of pure argument. Luther is a striking illustration of the supporting power of an angry temper. Being angry he forgot that he ever heard the name of death.

"When I get angry, I forget for the time my physical maladies. My understanding seems sharpened. I never speak better than when I am in a passion."

One of our preachers says his "faults are not worth mentioning." But that is just what they are. They are indispensable to the understanding of him. So are any man's; they make his virtues powerful. His morbidity gave vigor to his brain and sting to his diction. His perceptive faculties were sharpened by a disordered nervous organization.

He says, "The fault is mainly in those who knowing the irritability of the dog, persist in teasing him." He had a good heart but a bad temper, which is better than to have a bad heart and a good temper.

He would consent to no alliance with Zwingli or Calvin. The Reformer of Germany had no dealings with the Reformers of England, showing how little the "Lord's anointed" are anointed by his Spirit. Luther was as intolerant toward those who dared to go farther than he did, as the pope was toward those who went as far as Luther did. There was more than a jest in his jocosely calling himself the German pope. Luther revolted against

Another Turning-point

the intolerance of the pope, and was excommunicated for it; Zwingli revolted against the intolerance of Luther, and was repudiated for it.

He was horrified at the bloody deeds that followed his revolution, but he was not averse to putting a stop to a heretic by putting an end to his existence. He believed in the right of the State to punish heresy and advocated the burning of witches.

"I would have no compassion on these witches; I would burn them all."

He uses the same language in speaking of the peasants, the vicious Papists, the turbulent Swiss, Erasmus, and the witches; they should all be disposed of without mercy or toleration; they deserve the wrath of God and man—God and his vicegerent Luther. He speaks as having no power to do wrong.

Now look back to the emotional turbulence in the convent when he set about making Martin Luther a better man, and his church a better church, and his world a better world. Did he make himself a

The Human Martin Luther

better man? Did he not confound feeling right with doing right? feeling religious, with being religious? Was ever a man made better by a religious St. Vitus dance? Did he make his church a better church and his world a better world? I think he did—or if he did not his movement did.

He was no more under the influence of Jesus when he used such language, than Jesus was under Luther's influence when he commanded Peter to put up his sword, or us to obey the Golden Rule. Was ever a man thrown into an epileptic fit by reading the Sermon on the Mount?

Looking back now over these four hundred years, how far did he get? The pope held that there was no salvation outside of his church; Luther held that there was no salvation outside of his. He believed in transubstantiation, or the real presence, to the last. His theology was made up of slashing rationalism and rank sacramentarianism. He denounced the pope for setting himself above Scripture, and then set himself above it.

How Far did he Get?

He discredited the Epistle of Jude and the Epistle to the Hebrews.

He said that every man is at liberty to treat the Apocalypse according to the dictates of his own mind, and the German professors do so treat that and every other book at this day. He said that if the story of Jonah were not in the Bible, he would laugh at it, and that the whale could have digested Jonah in three days.

He repudiated the Epistle of James because it contradicted that of Paul in the matter of faith and works—another proof that his "The just shall live by faith," was a controversial cry rather than a definite conviction.

He questioned the infallibility of his new authority, the Bible, as stoutly as he did that of his old authority, the pope. He used his reason and extolled its use, but he denied its use to others.

Congregationalists will find no Congregationalism in Luther. He had no partiality for juvenile suffrage as a policy of the church. He would substitute the German emperor for the Roman pontiff. The destiny of the children which Jesus took such pains to make plain, has ever since been the despair of the ecclesiastics.

The pope would damn an infant Protestant, water or no water; Luther would save all the infant Protestants and Catholics if they would only stay long enough in the world to be baptized in it. He held with Augustine that we are born lumps of perdition, and if we should die in the act of being born we should as a logical—theological—desert of that act, go straight to hell for the glory of God.

He says: The human will is like a beast of burthen. If God mounts it, it goes as God wills; if Satan mounts it, it goes as Satan wills. Nor can it choose its rider. The riders, God and the devil, contend for its possession.

He gave an impulse to the human mind which it will never cease to feel, and yet his theory of its dependence would paralyze it forever. He was the founder of Protestantism, but it is doubtful whether one-tenth of the Protestants of to-day would acknowledge his authority in the-

Protestantism Leads to Evils

ology, and he would not recognize the Lutheranism of the present Germany. If the world had not gone beyond Luther both Luther and Protestantism would have been a failure.

But let us show him the fair play which he would show if he had lived in 1883 instead of in 1483. It is not to our credit or to his discredit that he lacked what we have, time, four hundred years of it. Another four hundred years, and we will have said of us what we say of him, and of Leo X.; they were out just four hundred years.

Those four hundred years past and these four hundred years to come, and all the years, are bringing us back, back, back to the words of Luther's Master and ours, who will be the world's Master yet.

Monseigneur Capel says Protestantism has led to evils, *i. e.*, evils to Monseigneur Capel. What then has he to say of Catholicism, which has led to the greatest of evils in his estimation, Protestantism?

So did the invention of money, which is a root of all evils; and printing—it has done more harm than smallpox, and smallpox is innocence in comparison with some Protestants and some Catholics.

Nevertheless we are in favor of the newspapers, and money—if one or two men do not get the whole of it—and Protestantism, which insures a fair hearing to all the gods and goddesses that are coming down on us from the English Olympus to poke fun at our Anglican snobbery and lead us in the way of sweetness and light.

Luther had to contend with sourness and darkness, not to speak of King Henry VIII., Defender of the Faith, by authority of the pope.

Luther owed something of his success to his nationality. A German owes his getting on to his being a German; he has Northern blood in his veins and Viking iron in his blood. He is anthracitic; he burns slowly, but he burns forever. The rise of Protestantism came of its having its rise in Germany. Savonarola's movement

Failing Powers

failed because it started in Italy and in Savonarola. Calvin failed to carry the French partly because they were French, and partly because he was Calvin.

But German though he was, with the German brawn and stamina, Luther wore out like an American; only he wore out in spite of the climate; we are worn out and torn up by the climate. At sixty-three he said, "I am used up." Emperor William and Bismarck have far exceeded that, but they have had no such foes to fight as Luther had—conscience and that sort of thing. He met his last enemy as he had met every other, with a shrinking spirit and a resolute front. He said he could not see how Paul could feel about death so forcibly as he writes. He (Luther) could not believe with respect to death as stoutly as he preached, or as stoutly as people thought he believed.

What with his physical decline, the bloody deeds of fanaticism at Münster, the loose lives of many of his followers, and the dissension among them, Luther's great heart sinks within him, and he thinks, "the latter days of Christ have come, and the last grand assault of the devil" is about to take place.

His confidence in the devil disputes the ascendency with his faith in God, and he exclaims: "I ardently hope that amidst these internal dissensions, Jesus Christ will hasten the day of his coming and crumble the whole universe into dust."

"I am feeble and weary of life, and would fain bid adieu to the world which is given over to the evil one."

"Rather than live forty years I'd give up my chance of paradise."

He believes the world, like himself, is approaching its end. A friend says the Emperor Charles will live to eighty-four. Luther replies, "The world itself will not last so long. Ezekiel tells to the contrary. If we drive forth the Turk, the prophecy of Daniel will be fulfilled, and then you may rely on it, the day of judgment is at hand."

Over three hundred years have passed and the Turk has just made a pretty good

Falling Powers

fight of it, and there is no likelihood of his being driven forth.[1]

Luther lay down to die at Eisleben where he was born. He died in harness. He had come there to participate in a conference of his church which, now that he was dying, was only beginning to live. He preached four times, and revised some ecclesiastical regulations. He was an ecclesiastic to the last, and an ecclesiastic is industrious.

It was the evening of the seventeenth of February, 1546, more than three hundred years ago. He retired for the night, complaining of feebleness and pains and inability to sleep. "If I could only sleep," he said. They give him a soothing drug. He slept, slept, and wakened and prayed. He told the watchers to "pray that the gospel may extend, for it is menaced by the pope and the council of Trent."

He repeated according to the German

---

[1] In this year (1897) he has made a still better fight than against Russia in 1883. But as many of the evils deplored by Luther came from the division among Protestants, so the Turk's triumph to-day has come because of the lack of European concert [ED.].

custom, three times the words, "Into thy hands I commend my spirit. Thou hast redeemed me, O Lord God of truth."

His eyes closed suddenly, and he swooned away, but the physicians succeeded in reviving him, and he took one more look on his friends and family.

He was asked, "Do you die firm in the faith you have taught?" He opened his eyes wide and looked intently upon the old friend who asked the question, and answered it in one word, "Yes." It was his last word. There could be no last word more becoming to Martin Luther.

He said, "Yes," and fell asleep. The soul of the mighty leader and Protestant came back to answer to all the world and for all time, "Yes." Martin Luther stood firm.

He became paler and paler, and colder and colder; his pulse ceased, his breath ended with one deep sigh, and his sighing ended forever, reminding us of one of his most striking and searching utterances, "Our faith is an unutterable sigh."

1. The Roman Catholic Church has not regained any nation, or any of the territory it lost four hundred years ago.

2. It has lost since then what gave it half its hold, the temporal power. The papal State has disappeared.

3. It has virtually surrendered in every contest with science. St. George Mivart and Professor Proctor would not have been tolerated by Leo X., nor would he have put a cardinal's cap on Newman's head. Leo XIII. represents quite another age. The stars in their courses have won in their fight with the papacy that destroyed Galileo, who was right; the church moves as well as the world. The church moves because the world moves.

4. Protestantism as a system has made no more progress in Catholic countries than Catholicism has in Protestant countries.

5. Protestantism has gained one nation, and a powerful one. This is the most formidable claim that either party can make for these four hundred years.

6. However, we should bear in mind that this Protestant nation was created by emigration, developed by moderation, not by conflict as Germany was, and the Protestant majority makes no progress with the Catholic minority or the Catholic minority with the Protestant majority. But the Catholicism of this country has not the grip of that of Italy or France, and that of France and Italy is not that of France and Italy in Luther's times.

7. The disintegrated Protestant Germany of Luther, has been consolidated into the first nation of the continent. The Luther celebrations in Germany now are not religious or ecclesiastical, but political, the jubilation of a political power of which Luther never dreamed; but Luther unwittingly laid its corner-stone.

8. The Lutheran branch of Protestantism is the farthest from being alive of any branch of it. The Roman Church shows more life at its extremities than Luther's church does at its heart.

9. Catholicism has just as much missionary activity as Protestantism.

10. In comparing the two forms of Christianity, Catholicism and Protestantism, we should bear in mind that Catholicism has no discussion within itself,[1] Protestantism carries with it many questions, serious and frivolous, ecclesiastical, theological, moral, and social, that are grinding on one another and must be settled with. We are necessarily retarded by the temporary consequence of a right position; they are helped by the temporary advantage of a wrong position. Give us time enough and the day is ours. The present is on their side; the future is on ours. Protestantism has nothing to fear from Romanism but something to fear from—Protestantism.

11. As neither Romanism nor Protestantism is what it was in Luther's day, the final result in the far future will not be the Protestantism or the Romanism of our day.

---

[1] This can hardly be said at the present time (1897), at least in this country. As is well known there is a very distinct divergence of opinion between Archbishop Ireland and Archbishop Corrigan. The truth seems to be that there is more unity among Protestants than appears, and far less among Roman Catholics [ED.].

12. In that final result we shall have no part or lot. We are not responsible for the four hundred years past or the four hundred years to come. We are only responsible for a few brief years, each for his own conscience, to his own conscience, for what that conscience requires him to believe and to be.

Yes, Martin Luther's followers stand firm by the logic of his teachings; the inalienable right of every conscience to have its own creed, or to have none, with no other conscience daring to molest or make it afraid, and that without the Christian's morality there can be no such thing as the Christian religion, and without religion, no religious authority can be accepted.

"Here we take our stand. We can do no otherwise," and we found our confidence in the future of our cause on the noble sentiments of Luther's hymn:

> A safe stronghold our God is still,
> A trusty shield and weapon;
> He'll help us clear from every ill
> That hath us now o'ertaken.

With force of arms we nothing can,
　　Full soon were we down trodden;
But for us fights the proper man,
　　Whom God himself hath bidden.

Ask ye, who is this same?
Christ Jesus is his name,
The Lord Sabaoth's Son;
He and no other one,
Shall conquer in this battle.

JOHN WESLEY

II

THE name of the man who founded the Methodist Church is John Wesley. The man who did that deserves to be studied. It will interest and instruct us to make a study of his biography.[1]

His Parentage

Where was he born? At Epworth, England. When was he born? In 1703. When did he die? In 1791.

His father, rector of the English church at Epworth, seems to have been a good and faithful father, but his mother had the first fashioning of the boy Jack, as he was called, and gave him his first impressions, ideas, thoughts, impetus. Susannah Wesley, mother of John and Charles Wesley, and seventeen others—let us speak of her with reverence and think of her as one of the great women, and one of the mighty mothers in Israel.

---

[1] I shall follow Tyerman's "Life and Times of Wesley."

John Wesley

She ruled well her own household. She taught John Wesley at one year of age that he had a right to cry, but that he had no right to bawl and yell and scream. This was tact. She taught self-restraint at one year of age. She never gave her children what they cried for. They were washed and put to bed at eight o'clock, after they had said the Lord's Prayer. She nipped all rudeness and selfishness in the bud. She acted upon the proverb, "A child left to himself bringeth his mother to shame" (Prov. 29 : 15).

At six years of age John was plucked as a brand from the burning parsonage. At eight years of age he came near dying of smallpox.

He spent five years at a good school in London, during which time he never had a mouthful of food more solid than bread. Why? Because it was the custom for the older boys to take not only their share of the meat, but the share of the younger boys also.

Early Life

Little England is a little pig—ditto, little America. This is one of the evidences that we are evolved from pigs—we behave so like them.

At this London school he attracted attention by qualities for which he was afterward famous—industry and persistency and the remarkable patience with which he bore insult and injuries. While his elders were knocking him around and stealing his meat, he treated his juniors to an oration. He was fond of getting them together and haranguing them. When asked by his teacher why he preferred the society of his inferiors to that of his equals among the boys, his reply was, "Better to reign in hell than serve in heaven."

He went from the London school to Oxford University. He was entitled to forty pounds a year for having attended this school, the Charterhouse; such schools are the glory of England. His entrance was obtained by the Duke of Buckingham. Here he was at Oxford University, twenty-one years of age, in poor health and in debt, bleeding at the nose and bleeding at the pocket. And here comes a letter from his mother—no money in it. She had none to give. Her husband had been in prison for debt. Her boy had been entered at the London school as the son of an impoverished clergyman.

But the words of a mother to her boy—they are "apples of gold in pictures of silver."

DEAR JACK: I am uneasy because I have not heard from you.

Aye, uneasy lies the head that wears the crown of motherhood.

Inform me of the state of your health and whether you have any reasonable hopes of being out of debt. I am most concerned for the good, generous man that lent you ten pounds, and am ashamed to beg a month or two longer, since he has been so kind as to grant us so much time already. We were amused by your uncle's coming from India, but I suppose these fancies are laid aside.

I wish there had been anything in it, for then perhaps it would have been in my power to have provided for you. But if all things fail I hope God will not forsake us. We have still his good providence to depend on.

Dear Jack, be not discouraged. Do your duty.

His Companions

Keep close to your studies and hope for better days. Perhaps after all we shall pick up a few crumbs for you before the end of the year.

Dear Jacky, I beseech Almighty God to bless thee.

SUSANNAH WESLEY.

When she was dying she said, "Children, as soon as I am released, sing a song of praise."

At twenty-four years of age we find him shaking off uncongenial acquaintances and choosing only such as were in accord with his spiritual-mindedness.

He says that when he resolved to be not a nominal but a real Christian, he found that his acquaintances were as ignorant of God as he was. Only he knew his own ignorance and they did not know theirs. Even their harmless conversation damps his good resolutions.

So he ceased to return their visits and their visits ceased. That was the right way. When you pray to be delivered from evil, answer your prayer by keeping out of evil company. If you would not be led into temptation, do not allow yourself to be led into the society of the tempter.

At twenty-four years of age he became curate to his father, who was sixty-five and palsied.

One of his earliest sermons is characteristically outspoken and plain-spoken. He reproves those preachers who wash their hands of stubborn texts that will not bend to their purpose, or texts that too plainly touch upon the reigning vices of the places in which they preach. His congregation is described as "unpolished wights, as dull as asses, and impervious as stones." It may be easy enough to find sermons in stones, but it is not so easy to preach sermons to stones.

At twenty-six he became a tutor in the University of Oxford, and here began what is called the "Methodist Movement." The place was Oxford, England, the time, 1729.

The Methodist Movement

It was begun by Charles, not by John. Charles Wesley was a fellow of Christ

College. He had suddenly turned from a life of frivolity to one of pious observances. He left his frolicsome behavior and began to attend the communion with great regularity.

His brother John joined him, as did a few others. Their regularity, so conspicuous in the midst of a universal irregularity, drew the name "Methodists," and says John Wesley, "As the name 'Methodist' was new and quaint, it clave to them immediately and from that time." He says it was given in allusion to an ancient sect of physicians who taught that almost all diseases might be cured by a specific method of diet and exercise.

The name was used in England long before it was applied to Wesley and his friends. In a sermon preached in 1639, the preacher exclaimed, "Where are now our plain packstaff Methodists, who esteem all flowers of rhetoric in sermons no better than stinking weeds."

If there be "Methodists," or any others, who so esteem the flowers of rhetoric, they are wrong. Jesus Christ used a flower of rhetoric when he said, "Behold the lilies of the field."

Whatever be the origin of the word, there is no doubt of its being applied to Charles Wesley's following at Oxford, or its becoming then and there and thenceforth a name of inextinguishable power and imperishable honor. So, as the first disciples of Christ were called Christians in derision at Antioch, the first to lift up a standard against the license of the church of that day were derisively called Methodists at Oxford.

While the first step and stand were taken by Charles, the leadership fell upon John, for the very simple reason that John was a born leader and Charles was not; John was the founder of the Methodist Church.

At this period John Wesley was twenty-six years of age, and is described as having an air of authority, but not of arrogance. He was handsome and spiritual-looking; his hair was long and silken; his eye sparkled with benevolence and decision blended.

His Personality

His Personality

The impress of his glorious mother was upon him. He was such a gentleman as only such a mother can train. A movement which was destined to surpass all other Protestant movements in taking hold of the ignorant masses was begun by a man of the highest education. The man who founded the Methodist Church was a learned man, a scholar, a school-made man as distinguished from what is called a self-made man. Every man is a self-made man who makes the most of his circumstances.

As we have seen, Methodism was organized in 1729. In 1733 there were twenty-seven Methodists, followers of Wesley, at Oxford. These were soon reduced to five, and but for John Wesley they would have been reduced to nobody.

It is interesting to note the constancy and persistency of Wesley, at thirty years of age, in contrast with the inconstancy of his followers. They were perpetually falling away or running away; they had not the root of the matter in them.

Wesley attributes his first spiritual impulse to the Moravians and obtained his first idea of a religious organization from them. While the germ was Moravian, the modifications and the additions were such as circumstances and his own sagacity suggested. The Methodist class was suggested by the Moravian band. Indeed Wesley established both band and class.

The movement was no sooner under way than the wicked rose up against it and the righteous took counsel against it.

At Bristol, England, while he was preaching the mob shouted, cursed, and swore around the place. A Catholic priest in the congregation cried out, "Thou art a hypocrite, a devil, an enemy to the church!" A curate of the Church of England, on the other hand, published him as a Papist. The bells were rung to drown his voice.

Mobbed

He was refused admittance to the sacramental table of the Church of England, together with his brother Charles and their converts.

Mobbed

At Pensford a bull was forced among the people, and the table on which Wesley stood was torn to atoms by the savages. At Whitechapel a herd of cattle was driven among the worshipers. At Cardiff, while Charles Wesley was preaching, women were kicked, and their clothes were set on fire by the rockets thrown into the congregation. The Bible was wrested from the preacher's hands, one of the mob declaring that he would persecute the Methodists to his dying day, if he had to go to hell for it (as he probably did). The houses in which the preachers lodged were assaulted and the windows smashed in. At Hampton women were pulled downstairs by the hair of their heads, and men were thrown into a hole full of noisome reptiles. A ruffian struck him on one cheek and he turned the other also, which so abashed the ruffian that he dropped his head and skulked away.

At Wolsal John Wesley was completely in the hands and power of the mob, and it is marvelous that he escaped alive. He was struck several times with an oaken club. One struck him on the breast, and another on the mouth with such force that the blood gushed out. He was dragged through the streets and pulled by the hair, one man exclaiming, "What soft hair he has!"

He asked them if they were willing to hear him speak, whereupon they shouted: "No, no; knock out his brains. Down with him! Kill him!"

Wesley asked: "What evil have I done? Which of you all have I wronged in word or deed?" Then he began to pray, and just then the ringleader of the mob turned suddenly in his favor and delivered him. "Follow me," he said, "and no man shall hurt a hair of your head."

This man was so impressed with Wesley's appearance and behavior that he not only delivered him out of the hands of the mob but afterward became one of his followers and lived to the age of eighty-five in the fear of God, and was always telling how God stayed his hand when it was lifted against Wesley's life. When he was asked what he thought of Wesley

Mobbed

during the assault, he replied: "I thought he was a man of God and God was on his side, when so many of us could not kill one man."

Of the same peril Wesley himself says: "A little before ten o'clock God brought me safe to Wednesbury, having lost one flap of my waistcoat, and a little skin from one of my hands. It came into my mind, that, if they should throw me into the river it would spoil the paper in my pocket. For myself, I did not doubt that I should swim across, having but a thin coat and a light pair of boots."

A woman who had been one of his converts fell away and turned so against him that she resolved to do him an injury. She accordingly invited him to her house, threw him down and cut off his long beautiful locks on one side. And so he appeared in the pulpit, those who sat on his cropped side wondering at his taste, and those who sat on the other side not knowing that he had been cropped.

Then the Pilate of the State joined hands with the Herod of the Church, and

John Wesley and his friends were charged by the civil authority with inciting the disorders of which they were the victims, and arraigned before the magistrates. At one place a wagon-load of Methodists were carried before a magistrate, who asked what they had done. Then some one said: "They have converted my wife. She used to have such a tongue! Now she is as quiet as a lamb." Whereupon the magistrate replied: "Take them away and let them convert all the scolds of the town."

Opposition of the State

The Church of England pulpits were closed against him, and clergymen of the Church of England who affiliated with Wesley were insulted during the service.

The Rev. Charles Manning's churchyard was used for fighting cocks. People turned their backs upon him while he was reading prayers or preaching. His choir was obstreperous—the only obstreperous choir I ever heard of. One man came into the church during the service with a pipe in his mouth and a pot of beer in his

Matrimony

hand. Some sat in the belfry ringing the bells and spitting on the heads of the worshipers.

He was pursued with what he describes as "pious venom." Every conceivable variety of calumny was set afloat against him by some of his own household of faith, of whom he exclaims: "And yet these are good Christians, these whisperers, talebearers, backbiters, evil speakers. Just such Christians as murderers and adulterers." Backbiters and murderers classed together! The worst of these backbiters who tried to murder him was his wife.

You have heard of his matrimonial misadventure. He married a widow and caught a Tartar. And her tart reflections, he says, "Like drops of eating water on the marble, at length have worn my spirits down." Yet he says he could not say, "Take thy plague away from me," but only, "Let me be purified, not consumed."

She proceeded to purify him by tearing

his hair out by the fistful. She was once caught by one of Wesley's friends in the act of dragging him about the floor by the hair of his head. She made accusations against him of the most villainous and calumnious kind, but not a particle of the mud sticks to his name.

She signs her letters: "Your affectionate wife," and her tombstone says, "She was a woman of exemplary piety."

But then you know a tombstone is like a corporation—it has no body to be burned or soul to be damned. I heard lately of a church that starved their preacher to death and are now collecting for his monument. He asked for bread and they gave him a stone—a tombstone.

The widower of this specimen of exemplary piety says he believed the Lord overruled this painful business to his good. "If she had been a better wife I might have been unfaithful in the great work to which God has called me." But I have a higher opinion of John Wesley than to think his fidelity to his work depended upon his having his hair pulled by a vicious wife,

Matrimony

and a higher opinion of Divine Providence than to think he would require such penance. He might well thank God for making him an itinerant preacher, with such "a charge to keep" as he had.

He wrote in favor of celibacy.

Nothing could daunt the purpose or dampen the ardor of the glorious man who founded the Methodist Church.

He had a lamblike spirit, but he was lion-mettled. Once when driving to a preaching appointment, they came to where the sands were overflowed and perilously deep with water. The driver hesitated, but Wesley put his head out of the window and exclaimed, "Take the sea, take the sea," and in they went. The driver who tells the story, says that he expected to be drowned.

Wesley asked, "What is your name, driver?"

"Peter."

"Peter, fear not; thou shalt not sink."

And they did not, but passed safely over, and Wesley, drenched to the skin, proceeded to fill his appointment.

No sooner did the attacks of the mob cease than he was attacked by a fever. The physicians told him he must rest. Wesley replied that he could not, because he had several appointments and must preach as long as he could speak. And off he went, but down he came. For three days he lay more dead than alive. His tongue swelled, his pulse could not be felt; his convulsions were violent. His friends abandoned hope. Six days afterward he was up and at it again. He was then seventy-two years of age.

His Consuming Zeal

He says of himself, "I can face the north wind at seventy-seven better than I could at twenty-seven." "I do not admire fair-weather preachers."

Like Luther, Wesley was very fond of music. Indeed all the Wesleys were, for it was a passion in the family. He attended the oratorio performances and listened to them with rapture, and criticised their performers wherein he considered them at fault.

But his greater passion was evident here

too. He reveled in the religious sentiment of the famous oratorios and thought this sentiment joined with the music might make an impression upon even rich and honorable sinners.

Never was a man more appropriately called a "Methodist," if that designation turns upon the word and article of method. A more methodical man never lived. He ran all to method, intellectually, personally, and religiously. He was as methodical as a clock. He said: "Any time for doing a thing was no time for doing it."

He wrote by method, talked by method, walked by method, went to bed and rose by method. His religious devotions were performed with all the regularity known to a convent, and his secular duties were as rigidly conformed to a system as are those of a military camp.

It came of the structure of his mind, the necessity of his nature; it made the type of his religion. Formal observance was both the cause and the effect of spiritual life.

He enjoins his followers: "Let all of you meet in band. As soon as the assistant has fixed your band make it a point of conscience never to miss without an absolute necessity. If you constantly meet your band, I make no doubt that you will constantly meet your class. Whoever misses his class twice together thereby excludes himself, and the preacher ought to put out his name."

His catechism of his preachers was close and rigid.

"Do you rise at four?

"Do you pray at five?

"Do you recommend the five-o'clock hour for private prayer?

"Do you fast once a week?

"Do you constantly attend the church and sacraments?

"Do you know the Methodist doctrine and the Methodist plan?

"Do you know the rules of the society and the bands? Do you keep them?

"Have you considered the twelve rules of a helper, especially the first, tenth, and twelfth, and will you keep them?

"Will you preach every morning and evening, endeavoring not to speak too loud or too long, not lolling with your elbows?

"Have you read the 'Rules for action and utterance'?

"Will you meet the society, the bands, the select society, and the leaders of bands and classes in every place?

"Will you diligently and earnestly instruct the children and visit from house to house?

"Have you read the 'Minutes' and are you willing to conform to them?

"Have you read the 'Sermons' and the 'Notes on the New Testament,' the 'Plain Account' and the 'Appeals'?

"Do you take snuff, or tobacco, or drams?"

To a preacher in Ireland he wrote: "Use all diligence to be clean. Whatever clothes you wear let them be whole: No rents, no tatters, no rags. Mend your clothes, or I shall never expect to see you mend your lives. Let none ever see a ragged Methodist. Clean yourselves of lice and the itch, you and your families. A spoonful of brimstone will cure you of the itch."

He not only abstained from the use of spirituous liquors except as medicine, but he denounced them as liquid fire, and those who sell them, except for medicine, as poisoners and murderers.

He published in 1760, "Advice to Methodists with regard to Dress." He would not advise them to imitate the Quakers in those little particularities of dress which can answer no possible end but to distinguish them from other people. To be singular merely for singularity's sake is not the part of the Christian. He did advise them to imitate the Quakers in the neatness and plainness of their apparel. He disapproved of velvets, silks, fine linen, jewelry, earrings, finger rings, necklaces, lace, ruffles, and all ornamentation.

Concerning Dress

"Wear nothing of a glaring color, nothing made in the height of fashion, nothing apt to attract the eyes of bystanders."

Concerning Dress

The biographer asks, "What will the fashionable followers of Wesley say to this?" They may say that if any costume of that period, or of this, is calculated to attract the eyes of bystanders, it is that of those who array themselves in the height of the fashion dictated by John Wesley or George Fox.

If these are not particularities of dress which distinguish the wearers from all other people, and make them singular, for singularity's sake, there is nothing in the way of costume that can accomplish that object. Moreover, the fact is that that object was accomplished. The costume of the followers of Wesley made them conspicuous and singular, as the costume of the followers of George Fox made them conspicuous and singular.

There is just as much singularity in being extremely unfashionable as there is in being extremely fashionable. Both are extremely foolish. There is just as much vanity under a religious costume as there is under an unreligious or an anti-religious costume.

There are two classes of people who should say nothing about their own piety; those who have some, and those who have none. Piety will speak for itself, if one has any to speak of.

In answer to those preachers who said they had no taste for reading, Wesley said, "Contract a taste for it, or return to your trade." To those who complained that they had no books, he offered to give books to the value of five pounds.

They were to give special attention to the children, for whom he wrote a volume called "Instructions for Children." "I reverence the young, because they may be useful after I am dead."

To those who said, "I have no gift for this," he replied, "Gift or no gift, you are to do it, else you are not called to be a Methodist preacher."

John Wesley did not believe that ignorance was the mother of devotion. So far from believing that, he looked upon it as the enemy of devotion, and made war upon it as such.

He set an example of industry and as-

His Self=denial

siduity rarely to be met with in history, and insisted that his preachers should follow his example. They read and studied systematically, daily, and imparted their information to others. He told his preachers to spend at least five hours in the twenty-four in reading the most useful books. He made short and sharp work of the plea that only the Bible should be read. He calls this, "rank enthusiasm," and instances a man who began by reading only the Bible and ended by reading neither the Bible nor any other book. He told his preachers that if they needed no book but the Bible, they had gotten beyond Paul; he needed other books.

The self-denial of the man who founded the Methodist church is worthy the admiration and imitation of all who belong to that or any other church. He did not call upon others to do what he would not do himself; he did not persuade others to give, give, give, and never give a penny himself.

All great religious movements have been marked largely by the benevolent element; almsgiving, helping the helpless and giving to the poor. The orders of the Catholic Church make much of this. The Ritualists of England make no less of it. All religious brotherhoods and sisterhoods are devoted to this idea of benevolence, even to making it a penance and a sacrament and a work meet for repentance.

The Methodist movement turned to the poor and destitute at once. John Wesley sacrificed his own ease and comfort at once for their sake. He says he gave away all that was left after providing for his own necessities. When he received thirty pounds a year he gave away all over twenty-eight, when he received sixty and ninety and one hundred and twenty pounds a year, he continued to live on twenty-eight, and gave the rest to the poor.

Wesley was as careful to be no financial burden to his hearers as was the Apostle Paul. He made no charge and received no salary, and there was no dodge or fraudulent pretention to superi-

His Self=Denial

ority in this. Salary was recompense, and anything in the way of recompense was salary.

A lady presented him with a chaise and a pair of horses and left him a legacy of one thousand pounds, but it was soon gone, given to the poor. His poor sister, who had been deserted by what some people call a husband, her natural protector, applied for some of it, but she was too late. He writes:

"Dear Patty, you do not consider; money never stays with me; it would burn me if it did. I throw it out of my hands lest it should find a way into my heart."

He was once too poor to get his hair cut. He became the proprietor of a large book concern, whose profits were also given away in charity and for the benefit of the cause he loved so well. There is good authority for the statement that he gave away more than one hundred and fifty thousand pounds after he had established his own book concern.

He tells his followers: "If you are

not in pressing want give something. If you earn but three shillings a week and give a penny of it, you will never want." He says he is ashamed of their penuriousness if they are not, and that if every one would give according to his means there would be money enough to meet all the necessities of all the societies. So it is now. He detested rich and stingy Christians.

At the conference of 1766 we find the soul of the man who founded the Methodist Church hectored with church debts. The debts on the one hundred chapels throughout the kingdom amounted to nearly sixty thousand dollars. Wesley said: "We shall be ruined if we go on thus." Ruined! Why, bless thy devout soul, Saint John, we disciples of the meek and lowly Jesus thrive and flourish on a debt twice as large as that, on one church, the Church of the Blessed Mortgage.

Church Debts

He writes to one preacher, "You must go to York, Leeds, and Bradford. Our rich men subscribe twenty shillings a year, and neither Boardman, Bumstead, nor Oliver, can move them. They want a hard-mouthed man. I beg you either mend them or end them."

The difficulty is to either end them or mend them. One of them said: "True I do not give much, but if you knew how it hurts me to give that, you would not ask me for any more."

His three favorite rules, which he elaborated in one of his sermons, were, "Gain all you can," "Save all you can," "Give all you can."

In the spring of 1736 he landed in Savannah, Georgia, with his brother Charles and three other Methodists. Savannah then had forty houses. Georgia was a feeble colony, and the only foretaste of what we are now as a nation was to be found in the fact that the highest officeholder was accused of stealing the public money.

His success in Georgia seems to have been small. The Indians were obdurate and the colonists indifferent to his form of religion. Besides, the Moravians were before him there as in England, and were doing his work in very much his way. Worse than all, he got into several rows, a row with the ecclesiastical authorities, and a row with the civil authorities. The upshot of the broil was that Wesley escaped by night in a rowboat, and after many perils reached England.

Curiously enough, in Savannah, where both Wesley and Whitefield labored, Methodism has but a feeble hold, while the denomination planted then and there is the largest and the most nearly universal of any in the United States.

His wit was quiet but quick. With him wit and wisdom went together; it was witty wisdom and wise wit.

His Wit

Once, in the impatience that came of his marvelous industry, when kept waiting for his carriage he exclaimed, "I have lost ten minutes for ever."

A friend said, "You have no need to be in a hurry."

"Hurry! I have no time to be in a hurry!"

He said to one of his preachers,

Shall Women Preach?

"Tommy, touch that dock. Do you feel anything?"

"No."

"Now touch that nettle... Tommy, some men are like docks, stupid, insensible; others are like nettles—touch them and they resent it. You are a nettle, Tommy; but I would rather have to do with a nettle than a dock."

Once while sitting with some friends at the excellent dinner of a rich Methodist, a canting preacher rolled up his eyes and sighed and said to Wesley:

"O sir, things are very different from what they were formerly. There is very little self-denial among Methodists now."

Wesley replied, "My brother, here is a fine opportunity for self-denial."

We now come upon the question whether women have any right to go anywhere in the world and preach the gospel to any creature, in the shape of what the biographer first calls a "godly female," and then a "preacheress." He means a godly woman and good preacher by the name of Sarah Crosby, who says: "My soul was much comforted in speaking to the people, as the Lord has removed all my scruples respecting the propriety of my acting thus publicly." She may be the original of Dinah Morris in "Adam Bede."

Nothing so forcibly illustrates the reverence in which Wesley was held by his followers as the fact that this good woman and good preacher after having all her scruples about preaching removed by the Lord, writes to ask Wesley what he thinks of her conduct—in a word, if he concurs with the Lord.

Wesley's answer is worth your hearing. It is written with a caution which continues unto this day, and which very well represents the attitude of some toward the question in at least three great denominations.

"I think you have not gone too far,"—she had gone so far as to preach to several hundred people to their great delight and edification,—"you could not well do less." He tells her to tell them that she does not take upon herself any such character as

His Peculiar Type of Piety

that of a preacher, she just tells them what is in her heart. "I do not see that you have broken any law. Go on calmly and steadily."

She did go on till her death in 1804, when there were several women preachers. Such, says his biographer, "was the commencement of female preaching"; he means preaching by women among the Methodists. It was never sanctioned by Wesley's Conference, but was practised to the end of Wesley's life.

To another he says, her justification lies in her having what he had, "an extraordinary call."

"It is plain to me that the whole work of God termed Methodism is an extraordinary dispensation of his Providence."

He should have put his right to ordain the superintendents he sent to America on the same ground, and saved himself from an ecclesiastical tangle which is the only muddy spot in his clear head.

His peculiar type of piety I shall not go into in a controversial way. There are as many types of Christian piety as there are kinds of temperament, varieties of Christian culture, and schools of Christian exegesis. This must be acknowledged by all who acknowledge that George Fox was as clearly entitled to be called a Christian as John Knox, or Augustine as Luther, or Channing as Calvin, or Elizabeth Fry as Madame Swetchine, or John Wesley as Oliver Cromwell, or Dr. Peabody as Dr. Pusey.

John Wesley's Peculiar Type of Piety

Concerning one peculiarity of John Wesley's peculiar type of piety there can be no question, and with respect to it there can be no controversy. Whatever else his theory of holiness meant, it meant, keep your fingers out of your neighbor's pocket; whatever else his idea of perfection implied, it implied perfect honesty.

"Never think of being religious unless you are honest." "What has a thief to do with religion?" "It is high time to return to the plain word: He that feareth God and worketh righteousness is accepted of him."

His Peculiar Type of Piety

He believed in mixing politics and religion in such proportions as to give religion the ascendency and keep politics from putrefaction.

So you see that whatever else his perfectionism meant, it meant, keep your fingers out of your neighbor's pocket if you love your neighbor as yourself. Whoever it may designate as free from sin, it puts the brand of sinners deserving to be damned upon all venal politicians and corrupt officeholders, especially if they hold one office in the Church, and one in the State at the same time—a union of Church and State which does not seem to weigh very heavily upon the consciences of those American Christians who are conscientiously opposed to the union of Church and State.

His perfection included the perfect keeping of the Golden Rule, and excludes Christian bankers who receive the hard earnings of the poor one day and close their doors the next. In one of his addresses to his followers he exclaimed: "Who does as he would be done by in buying and selling? He who keeps not this law is written down a knave."

The ticket which John Wesley gave to the class meeting was written in these words by his own hand, "I believe the bearer to be one who fears God and works righteousness." But with all his plain preaching many would still profess religion and practise dishonesty.

Wesley noted what preachers do not make as much note of as they should. It is the small amount of accurate knowledge communicated by the preacher to his hearers. He was amazed at the ignorance of his hearers, on topics in which he took the greatest pains to instruct them.

"I study to speak as plainly as I can, yet I frequently meet with those who have been my hearers for many years, who are ignorant of the nature of repentance, faith, and holiness."

After all his plain preaching and explicit teaching he says most of them have a religion which consists of a sort of confidence that "Christ will justify them while they live to themselves."

As a Preacher

Wesley as a preacher is worthy of study. He was clear of ornament, direct, and lucid. He could be elegant and simple without being effeminate. His education was not an enervation. There is that strength in his language which is inseparable from the language of those who use language as a means to an end instead of as an end.

He was searching and severe without reveling in phraseological severity. He was too good a fisher of men to suppose that he could catch them with the mere terminology of professional preaching. Like his Master, he used his greatest severity on the most polished.

Once he preached to an audience of elegant rascals, "Ye serpents, ye generation of vipers, how can ye escape the damnation of hell?" He was told that that was suitable for Billingsgate. He replied: "In Billingsgate I should preach from the text, 'Behold the Lamb of God which taketh away the sins of the world.'"

He reveals knowledge of human nature

and tact in controlling it. Speaking of Billingsgate fish market, whence we get the word, Wesley and a friend were standing near it once while two women were bandying the worst epithets of the place, when his friend said, "Come, sir, let us go; I cannot stand this."

Wesley replied, "Stay, Sammy, stay and learn how to preach."

Wesley's movement, like those of Finney and other revivalists, was accompanied by physical and mental effects which are now generally regarded as not only unnecessary, but mischievous. There is no better evidence of their being both preventable and unnecessary than the fact that nothing of the kind has ever been seen at Mr. Moody's meetings, although they have been composed of the very class most fruitful in these spasms and convulsions.

Physical Effects of his Preaching

This movement, like every other religious movement, drew a certain temperament, attracted and repelled, fascinated and alienated, as it does to this day,

Physical Effects of his Preaching

and as every denomination does to this day.

John Wesley believed that no special form of church government is commanded in the New Testament, and was quite content to let every person be persuaded in his own mind as to which was best, or even to live and die good Christians without ever knowing which was best.

Wesley's movement differs from that of all great religious reformers in this: it was an attempt at a reformation without a secession. Herein it failed and herein Wesley was involuntarily and unconsciously inconsistent with himself. He says his design was to leave his followers in the lap of their mother, the Church of England. But his American followers had no mother. I have a lively appreciation of those who have a mother church, but I have more sympathy with those who have no mother church.

Wesley said he dared not separate from the Church of England; it would be a sin to do so; but it would be no less a sin for him not to vary from it in preach-

John Wesley

ing abroad, praying extempore, and organizing societies. His preachers were forbidden to baptize or administer the sacraments. They were extraordinary messengers of God, not to supersede the ordinary messengers, but to provoke them to jealousy.

But he did not stop there. His brother Charles implored him, as he implored his preachers, "In God's name, stop there." Charles and others, both in the English Church and among the Methodists, maintained that ordination was separation; but John Wesley could not see it in that light, although he seems to have foreseen its working, for he writes in 1786 at eighty-three years of age:

"The preachers of a dissenting spirit will probably after our death set up for themselves and draw away disciples after them."

To such preachers he unwittingly gave his sanction in the most effective and solemn manner. He ordained and set them apart as superintendents and thus qualified and authorized them to administer

Physical Effects of his Preaching

the sacraments to the fifteen thousand American Methodists. These were soon called bishops. The name of the office was changed but its nature remained the same, a superintendency. The number of bishops necessarily increased, also the number of those who intended to be, the Lord willing, and if they knew their own hearts.

Charles Wesley was right; ordination was separation. John Wesley had promoted what he dreaded. He set up the American Methodists, and they set up themselves. So that Wesley may be said to be the only involuntary founder of a great religious society the world has ever known. He builded greater than he knew.

Calvin did what he intended to do when he organized a Church and State of his own at Geneva; Luther rejoiced in leaving his reformation stamped with his name; Knox gloried in the separation and independence of Presbyterianism in Scotland; the English Church was a popular secession of national proportions; the boast of

John Wesley

Puritanism is that of a new sect in a new land; but Wesley's fame is that of the founder of an independent denomination as powerful to-day as any of these, who died denying its necessity and opposing its formation.

Tyerman calls Wesley the autocrat of the Methodists; and he certainly was. His reply to those who complained of this and wished to share in Methodist legislation, is interesting. It contains a history of his autocracy and of early Methodism as well, in a nutshell.

An Autocrat

"In November, 1738, several persons came to me in London and desired me to advise and pray with them. I said if you will come on Thursday night, I will help you as well as I can. More and more then desired to meet with them, till they were increased to many hundreds. Here commenced my power, namely, a power to appoint when and where and how they should meet, and to remove those whose life showed they had no desire to flee from the wrath to come."

The fact is, that authority with Wesley was an individuality and a necessity. He was one of those great men whose mental organization fitted them for doing what Divine Providence gave them an opportunity to do. He followed his bent in obeying his call.

His call was just what he regarded that of the women whom he encouraged to preach and that of his lay preachers, "an extraordinary call," and like all extraordinary calls it only comes to those who are extraordinarily adapted for obeying it.

John Wesley rises before us a religious force of marvelous quietness. He was a wonderful example of quietness and confidence. He studied to be quiet. The noise of his movement was made by his enemies, and with them rests the whole blame and shame thereof. His was the quietest exhibition of power of which we have any account. He brandished no sword whose glitter stirred the blood; he bestrode no war horse that neighed courage to its rider; he led no party whose cheers supported the spirits. He was no stormy and dramatic Luther. He was no Cromwell, putting his enemies to the sword in the name of the Lord. He was no Knox, tearing down churches to get rid of their members. He was no Calvin—he did not burn anybody for disagreeing with him.

The oak under which John Wesley preached his first sermon in America is still standing. The system which he there planted has struck its roots deep in the civilization of the republic, and its branches have gone out into all the land, and its leaves will be for the healing of the nations long, long after the oak in Georgia has fallen and disappeared.

Others may be named before him as theologians, as philosophers, as preachers; but no man of history had a more elevating and commanding character, a more Christlike life, and no man among them all produced a more enduring or more beneficent influence upon his fellow-men than the man who founded the Methodist Church.

Tyerman calls him, at eighty years of

His Death

age, "a flying evangelist." A flying evangelist at eighty years of age! Do we hear that? We who are forever complaining and whining over our poor little contemptible services, what do we think of that for zeal and consecration?

We have hurried through his glorious life, and now come to his glorious death. He died with his armor on. He died in the midst of the battle, at the head of his hosts, under the banner of the cross. It was more a translation than a death. He was eighty-eight years of age.

His beautiful face retained its beauty to the last, his eye its lustre, his form its symmetry, his spirits their elasticity, his intellect its vigor, his conscience its keenness, his heart its benevolence, his Methodism its fervor, his faith in Christ its steadfast zeal.

He tottered on the pulpit stairway, whereupon the whole congregation burst into tears.

He had his wish that he so often expressed in his favorite verses:

John Wesley

> Oh that without one lingering groan
> I may the welcome word receive,
> My body with my charge lay down,
> And cease at once to work and live.

But when he ceased to work he began to live. Both he and his work will live forever.

It was the morning of the first of March, 1791, when the messenger came for him and found him singing:

> I'll praise my maker while I've breath;
> And when my voice is lost in death,
> Praise shall employ my nobler powers;
> My days of praise shall ne'er be past,
> While life and thought and being last,
> Or immortality endures.

Utterly exhausted, but inexpressibly happy, he looked out upon the watchers standing around his bed, and said, "Pray and praise." They sank upon their knees and obeyed his request, then rose and bent over him. He shook hands with each and said farewell, but still he lingered.

The lingering sunset of that lofty life filled the room with light and peace.

His Death

He exclaimed, "The Lord of hosts is with us, the God of Jacob is our refuge. Pray and praise."

Again they fell on their knees around the chariot of the ascending Elijah, and again they rose and gathered around to listen to his parting words.

So the night wore away and the morning came—and joy cometh in the morning. It was the morning of an immortal day to him. He exclaimed, "I'll praise—I'll praise," and at last he said, "Farewell," and the chariot started.

His body has long since gone to decay in the midst of the great world of London, but the name which I there saw passing away with the crumbling stone, is written on the hearts of millions in imperishable reverence.

The church that was so cruel to herself as to close her pulpits against him, receives a monument to his memory in the most venerable of her cathedrals. So is his cause vindicated and his wrongs redressed.

By the humble grave in City Road, by

John Wesley

the marble medallion in Westminster Abbey, and above all by the vast instrumentality that he left behind to carry on his work, we are reminded of the man who founded the Methodist Church, gathered as wheat fully ripe and fully ready for the reaper.

> We bend to-day o'er a hallowed form,
>   And our tears fall quietly down,
> As we look again on the warrior face,
> With its tranquil peace and its patient grace,
>   And hair like a silver crown.
>
> We know through what labors his hands have
>   passed,
>   Through what rugged places his feet,
> And we joy in the presence of his brow so white,
> As radiant now with heaven's own light,
>   As it shines in the ripened wheat.
>
> Then faithfully toil that in death we may come,
>   Not only with blossoms sweet,
> Not bent with doubts or burthened with fears,
> Or with dead, dry husks of life's wasted years,
>   But laden with golden wheat.

NORMAN MACLEOD

III

THE great-grandfather of our subject, Donald Macleod, lived in the mountain solitudes of the Island of Skye, not far from Dunvegan Castle. *Genealogy* He was "a good man, and the first to introduce regular family worship." This grandfather was educated for the church, and became minister of the Highland parish which made the subject of "Reminiscences of a Highland Parish." He had a small salary and a large family.

Sixteen children were born in the manse; in the rugged and romantic home of Morven they had their "bringing up."

The minister's piety was earnest, healthful, and genial. He delighted to make all around him happy. The boys had their classics, and the girls their needlework, but there was no grudging of their enjoyments. "In the winter evenings," says his biographer, "the minister would tune his violin, strike up a swinging reel, and call on the lads to lay aside their books and the girls their sewing, and all would dance with a will to his hearty music." This was followed by family worship, which ended the day with its round of duties and pleasures.

One of these sixteen children was the father of our subject, in many respects his prototype. He had tact and common sense, pathos and humor, and few could resist the tenderness of his appeals from the pulpit.

In the excellent memoir of Norman Macleod written by his brother, Rev. Donald Macleod, and dedicated to their mother, then in her ninety-first year, we find that the mother was a powerful element in the formation of his character. She was a centennial growth of the most noble country of the thistle.

His Mother

The discipline of the children was left to his mother, who was their companion and instructor at home and their constant correspondent in later life. Dr. Macleod said:

"We were seldom formally lectured on the subject of religion, but a religious atmosphere was created which we unconsciously imbibed. . . My mother has been my best earthly friend, and God knows the heartfelt, profound veneration I have for her character.

"Were I asked what there was in my parents' teaching and training which did us all so much good, I would say it was love and truth. Our parents were both so real and human. There were no cranks, twists, crotchets, isms or systems of any kind. They gave us a blowing-up when needed, but passed by trifles, failures, and infirmities, without making a fuss.

"Christianity was taken for granted, not forced with scowl and frown. I never heard my father speak of Calvinism, Arminianism, Presbyterianism, or Episcopacy, or exaggerated doctrinal differences. He might have made me a slave to any ism. He left me free to love Christ and Christians."

In Scotland to this day the children are brought up by the parents; the parents are not brought up by the children. Parental authority is still maintained. Home discipline continues to be the corner-stone of public order.

Norman Macleod was born at Campbelltown, which lies at the head of the lake which runs into the long promontory of Kintyre. As the Highlands gave him his strong Celtic passion, so Campbelltown inspired him with sympathy for the sea and sailors. His temperament was quick, and a lively intellect he had from the start.

His Early Life

He quickly caught the spirit of all outward things in nature or character, and his power of mimicry and sense of the ludicrous were developed very early. Once when only six years of age he was ill and had leeches applied to him. He named the leeches after the leading characters of the town, and scolded or praised them according as they did their work well or not, in the voice of the person imitated.

His Early Life

At twelve years of age he was sent to school in the Highlands, "to be made a true Highlander of," as his father said, and there he felt the glory of the hills, that remained upon his spirit through life. He retained the romance and poetic inspiration of the Highland scenery, as who does not?

For lifting up one's thoughts and turning up the corners of one's mouth there is nothing like mountain scenery. These carry one's mind away from groveling parsimony, and one's body from the ague, and take him through nature up to Nature's God.

> For the strength of the hills we bless thee,
>   God, our father's God.
> Thou hast made thy people mighty
>   By the touch of the mountain sod.

He was a rollicksome, frolicsome boy, and his parents feared he would never be sedate enough to become a minister. His brother says: "They wrote him very gravely on the dangerous tendencies betrayed by his frolicsome disposition. . .

The noisy fun and ceaseless mimicry in which he indulged disturbed the very quiet of the Sabbath in his father's manse."

On page thirty-six of his biography, we find a letter from his father saying: "You carry this nonsense much too far, and I beg of you, my dear Norman, to check it. Cease your buffoonery and distortions of countenance, which are not only offensive but grievous."

One of the "Queer Characters," such as one meets in Scotland, and one that was a great source of amusement to young Norman, was "Old Bell" as he was called, author of Bell's Geography. He was a weaver of large intellect and considerable literary taste, and of an emphasis and originality not unworthy of Dr. Johnson. He said of a man who was perpetually parading his perfect assurance of salvation, "I never saw a man so sure of going to heaven and so unwilling to go to it." When he was dying a young preacher undertook to pray with him, but he made such a fist at it that old Bell exclaimed: "My man, no doubt you mean well; but you had better go home and learn to pray for yourself before you pray for other people."

At the university Norman was more interested in general literature than in the classical studies, in which he never excelled. Instead of turning aside to make himself an expert in the dead languages he kept on the way of his natural disposition and cultivated his liking for the living languages of Shakespeare and Wordsworth, who opened a new world to him. If he had attempted scholarship or set himself to make a student of himself, he would have failed.

A fellow-student writes: "I verily believe that Wordsworth did more for Norman, penetrated more deeply and vitally into him, than any other voice of inspired man... Norman was not much of a classical scholar. Homer and Virgil and the rest were not much to him. But I often thought that if he had known them ever so well in a scholarly way, they would never have so entered into his secret being and become a part of his very self."

He followed the fashion in going into ecstasies over Goethe and then—forgetting all about him. Shakespeare, however, he never deserted; he was too highly endowed himself with the dramatic passion. He reveled in Falstaff and acted him admirably.

When he came to study theology under Dr. Chalmers he felt at once and ever after the influence of that powerful man. Here is character molding character. It was one of those cases where the pupil is roused, stirred, plowed by the teacher. Excitation is often a greater mental force than information.

<small>Influence of Dr. Chalmers</small>

He went to school at Weimar, Germany. It was almost violent transition from the Edinburgh Divinity Hall, and Dr. Chalmers, and Scotch Presbyterianism, to Dr. Weissenborn, and the fashionable rationalistic life of the town that Thackeray so lovingly describes.

<small>Life in Germany</small>

He was passionately fond of music, sang well to the guitar, danced as well as a Scotchman can be expected to dance, and became like Thackeray and all the young bloods, fascinated with the Baroness Melanie, the court beauty.

But the Scotch stamina did not yield to the corrosive influence of the German atmosphere. Once a Scotchman always a Scotchman, once a Presbyterian always a Presbyterian; and when you find a simon-pure born Scotchman, and a bred-in-the-bone Presbyterian in one and the same man or woman, you have the most indigestible file that the devil ever attempted to gnaw.

There is no better stuff for making character out of. It is one of those hard substances that endure pounding and bear a polish at the same time. I have seen it in all its glory in Scotland and I was fascinated with it. Norman Macleod owed his safety amid the perils of fashionable life to the granite of his character, which he got from the granite of the Highlands and the granite of his religion.

Norman Macleod

He wrote to his mother the day after his twenty-second birthday: "A knowledge of the world either spoils a man, or makes him more perfect. I feel that it has done me good in a thousand ways. I have been made to look upon man as man." Here is one of the peculiarities that classify him. He belonged to that class of fishers of men who look upon man as fish to be caught by the net of the kingdom of God. He looked upon himself, the fisher, as very like the fish, of like passions and infirmities, not above them, but one of them, struggling up with them, tumbling back with them. One of the all kinds that are gathered by the net.

His brother's death was a turning-point in the life of Norman Macleod. His affection for his brother made his heart mellow and susceptible to religious impressions. At that bed of death he prayed aloud in the presence of others for the first time; from this incident he dated the commencement of earnest Christian life. Of this event he writes:

A Turning=Point in his Life

A Turning-point in his Life

"I think I may defy time to blot out all that occurred at that time. That warm room, the large bed with blue curtains, the tall thin boy with the pale face, and jet-black sparkling eyes and long curly hair; the anxious mother, the silent steps. Then the loss of hope. The last scene. Oh, my brother; my dear brother; if thou seest me, thou knowest how I cherish thy memory. Yes, Jamie, I will never forget you. If I live to be an old man, you will be fresh and blooming in my memory." Here you have that ardent and profound sensibility which is a constituent element with joviality and good humor; they go together.

He was ordained and began to preach at the town of London, to a congregation made up of the most austere and the most lax in doctrine, Chartists and Tories and Covenanters, and all sorts politically, theologically, and socially. Partisan feeling ran high, so high as to create disturbance in the congregation, and the intruders had to be ejected by force. In his "Journal" he writes:

"I had Lord Jeffrey in church. I never had a more fixed and attentive listener. Luckily I was thoroughly prepared."

Young preachers soon learn, however, that they have nothing to fear from the bigwigs of their congregation. They know something of such difficulties from their own experience with the public. Those who are the best qualified for criticism are the least likely to display it.

He read a sermon in a district where the reading of a sermon was regarded as a serious offense. After the sermon, one old lady asked another if she did not think that a grand sermon.

"Aye, but he read it."

"Read it! I would not care if he whistled it."

He was a glorious preacher and platform speaker. I have heard and felt him, as he poured out his heart and soul and intellect upon the people. He gave me his friendship, and I knew him also as a sympathetic pastor and admirable organizer. He could keep several irons in the fire without allowing any of them to burn.

Preparing his Sermons

Speaking of sermon writing, he once said, "I never use a scrap of paper. I generally take eight hours to write a sermon. I never begin to commit until Saturday night. Four readings do it."

He was a thoroughly human and imperfect Christian, not an artificial one. He behaved like one. He did not study the part and act it. He did not adjust his attitudes, or arrange his countenance, or assume a phraseology, for the purpose of playing the character of a religious man or a minister. There was no "Uriah Heep" humility about him, or "Podsnappian" familiarity with the ways of the Almighty.

He says in one of his letters to a friend: "Oh, I hate cant! I detest it from my heart of hearts!"

In another letter: "I saw a tomb in the chapel of Holyrood with this inscription, 'Here lies an honest man.' I only wish to live in such a way as to entitle me to have such an epitaph." And he did so live.

But he kept a diary or religious log-book, which is not a healthful thing to do. You can put your pen to a better purpose. See that it does not make false entries in your account book, and let your guardian angel keep your log-book.

One of the many ecclesiastical revolutions that have overtaken Protestantism since the one that created it, was what is known as the "Disruption" in the Established Church of Scotland, in 1843, when four hundred and fifty ministers and elders and one hundred and fifty members marched out of the General Assembly and set up for themselves "The Free Church of Scotland."

The Disruption

Not to go into the controversy, which would take us too far from our main subject, suffice it to say that the dispute was over the jurisdiction of the State in the affairs of the church; or, in other words, over the spiritual independence of the church.

The two parties into which the church was divided had divergent beliefs as to

The Disruption

the nature of the spiritual independence which of right belonged to the church, so there was a division among them and subdivisions. There were Evangelicals, and Non-intrusionists, and Moderates—no immoderates in name, although a large number in behavior.

The two main divisions were the Established Church and the Free Church of Scotland, the latter founding itself on the principle of total independence of the State. Dr. Macleod remained in the old church and, as we might infer from his large and many-sided make up, looked out in a large, sanguine, rational way upon the whole conflict.

Writing to a friend he exclaimed, with his characteristic drollery: "Would we had an Inquisition. One glorious martyr fire would finish the whole question. . . The divine authority being stamped upon every leading ecclesiastic, everything in the civilized world must be overthrown which stands in the way of his notions being realized.

"There are ecclesiastics who look into

a glass and say, 'I see every time I look there one who always agrees with me.' That is their whole world. Of the rest they are profoundly ignorant.

"There are some men who, if left alone, are as cold as pokers, but like pokers, if they are once thrust into the fire, they become red hot, and add to the general blaze. Such are some ministers when they get into church controversies."

It is curious to notice the change in views that came over him with age and experience of the world. He says, "As to spiritual independence, in spite of all the courts can do, there is not a thing in God's word which I have not as much freedom to obey in the church as out of it."

He knew how to stay in a church with which he could not accord in every minute phase of opinion. He was not a schismatic or an ism-atic. "I thank God I was saved from the fearful excitement into which many of my friends were cast."

While he took sides, or rather remained

on the side of the old church, without regarding it as one of two sides, he was blind neither to her faults nor to the grand virtues of the seceders. He was not an irrational come-outer, neither was he an intolerant stay-iner.

He says: "As for church government I look upon it as a question of clothes—or rather of spectacles. What suits one eye will not suit another. What signifies whether a man reads with the spectacles of Episcopacy, Presbyterianism, or Congregationalism.

"Is it not a blessing that there is for one an old cathedral with stone knights and a bald-headed prelate, and for another a congregation that will listen to long metaphysical sermons, and that for another there is an Independent Church where he can fight the parson, and that in all they will hear what will make them wise unto salvation?"

In a letter to a friend he writes, "I value each form of church government in proportion as it gains the end of making man more meet for heaven.... At the same time I cannot incur the responsibility of weakening the Established Church, that bulwark of Protestantism, that breakwater against the waves of democracy and revolution, that ark of a nation's righteousness."

When he became chaplain to the queen he was not simply a formal hired chaplain to the royal household, he was a sympathetic and faithful pastor to them. He said to them: "I am here as a pastor, and as I wish you to thank me when we meet before God, so would I address you now."

Chaplain to the Queen

He wrote to his wife: "I spoke fully and frankly to the prince, when we were alone—of his difficulties, temptations, and what the nation expected of him. How if he did God's will, good and able men would rally around him; how if he became selfish, a selfish set of flatterers would truckle to him and ruin him, while caring only for themselves.

"The prince spoke to me about preaching only twenty minutes. I told him I was a Thomas à Becket and would resist the interference of the State, and that neither he nor any of the party had anything better to do than hear me. So I preached forty-seven minutes."

Thus you see he was no sycophant in the presence of royalty and I presume the queen liked him all the better for that. He was the confidential friend and adviser of the queen at the death of Prince Albert, and was admirably qualified by nature and religious manliness for the place.

He writes: "I am never tempted to conceal any conviction from the queen, for I feel she sympathizes with what is true and likes the speaker to utter the truth exactly as he believes it."

Again we find him suddenly in perils among his own brethren, when he took issue with his Presbytery on the Sunday observance question. The Presbytery sent a pastoral letter to its churches, basing the observance of Sunday on the laws and regulations of the Old Testament respecting the observance of the Jewish Sabbath.

He took the ground that the authority of the Jewish Sabbath was an insufficient, unscriptural, and therefore perilous basis, on which to rest the observance of the Christian Sunday. To use his own words: "It was charged that I gave up the moral law, when I merely denied that the moral law and the ten commandments were identical, and asserted that the moral law as such was eternal.

"That I did away with the Christian Sunday or Lord's Day when I denied that it rested as its divine ground on the perpetual obligation of the fourth commandment, but endeavored to prove its superior glory and fitness on other grounds.

"That I gave up the Decalogue as a rule of life, and therefore had no law to guide life, when I denied that we required to go to Moses for a rule, having Jesus Christ, and that the gospel was not a mere rule, but a principle, even life itself through faith in Christ."

Dean Stanley says he heard a Scotch-

The Sunday Controversy

man from Glasgow say in the railway carriage:

"Dr. Macleod is getting a fine heckling about the Doxology."

I presume this man came as near to the point at issue as many a one of those who disputed over it.

A conference was suggested to him and he replied, "Conference! And all because I do not find the whole moral law in the ten commandments, or because I think the Decalogue a covenant with Israel, and as such not binding on us, and I base the Lord's Day on Christ and not on Moses, and find Christ's teaching a sufficient rule of life, without the Mosaic Covenant."

These views were then quite common in all denominations and are far more common now. I read them in an editorial article of a leading denominational organ very recently.

"Yet," says his biographer, "if Dr. Macleod had renounced Christianity itself, he could scarcely have produced a greater sensation."

His table was loaded with letters remonstrating, abusing, denouncing, cursing. Ministers passed him without recognition; one of them hissed him on the street.

Writing of this time he says: "I felt so utterly cut off from every Christian brother, that had a chimney sweep given me his sooty hand, and smiled on me with his black face, I would have welcomed his salute and blessed him.

"Men apologized for having been seen in my company. An eminent minister refused to preach in a certain pulpit because I was to preach in it in the morning. Orators harangued against me in the City Hall.

"This was a terrible hurricane, but I had a stout heart, and, thank God, a conscience kept in perfect peace.

"Never have I experienced so much real, deep sorrow, never so tasted the bitter cup of enmity, suspicion, injustice and hate of ministers and members of the church.

"Oh, it was awful. One would have

The Sunday Controversy

to read the newspapers I have collected to comprehend the fury of the attack. Men from pulpits and press seemed to gnash their teeth upon me. Injustice, intolerance, misrepresentation, sneakiness make me half-mad; but the more need of silence, patience, and prayer."

His Presbytery admonished him and there the ecclesiastical part of the row came to an end, much to everybody's surprise, for the prisoner at the bar and everybody else expected to hear the storm howl in the General Assembly. Speaking after the manner of men, it was the merest chance whether the storm should go on or subside. Speaking after the manner of a Divine Providence the "remainder of wrath was restrained."

Dr. Macleod says he "did not recant or withdraw one word, but admitted to the Presbytery that he had taught against the Confession of Faith.

"I thus at the risk of my ecclesiastical life established the principle that all differences from the Confession did not involve deposition.

"In so far as the question of ministerial liberty was concerned, thank God, I have gained the day, and it is a bright day for Scotland, which will shine on unto the perfect day, which to me would be the subjection of every soul to the teaching of Jesus Christ, the one prophet of the church, and to Moses and the prophets as his servants, whose teaching is to be interpreted by that of the Master's."

He told the Presbytery that it "would be the last admonition they would address to a minister for preaching as he did, and he would show it to his son as an ecclesiastical fossil.

"Thank God, I am free. Never more shall I be trammeled by what partisan Christians think.

"One master, Christ, and his word, shall alone guide me, and speak I will when duty calls, come what may."

He said to me as we talked this battle over in his study, "If you ever take up the matter, you will see that justice is done me."

Very loyally and with a full heart will I

The Sunday Controversy

now speak for him and claim the justice he asked, simply the truth with respect to his opinions, which are to-day extensively received as in perfect accord with the teachings of him who alone has authority to teach the Christian religion.

His triumph was crowned by his unanimous election as moderator of the General Assembly in 1869. Instead of being driven from the church he was elevated to the highest position she had to confer. So the Philistines were subdued and came no more upon him there.

In the midst of the battle he addressed some ringing verses to his friend, Principal Tullock, who had made a stirring speech on his side.

> Brother, up to the breach
>   For Christian freedom and truth,
> Let us act as we teach,
>   With the wisdom of age and the vigor
>   of youth,
> Heed not their cannon-balls,
> Ask not who stands or falls,
>   Grasp the sword
>   Of the Lord,
>   And forward.

Norman Macleod

The day after his obnoxious speech on the Sunday observance question, he was told this story:

Origin and Object of the Starling   A very rigid Scotch clergyman had a very decent shoemaker for an elder who taught a favorite starling some old Scottish tunes. One Sunday morning the minister as he was passing heard the bird whistle "Over the Water to Charlie," and was so shocked that he told the elder he must wring the bird's neck or resign his office. The elder gave up his office and kept his starling and prospered.

The object of the story, he says, was to show the onesidedness and consequent untruth of hard logical principle when in conflict with genuine moral feeling. This story gave great offense to the intolerant portion of the Scotch Church.

He was fond of his home and a companion to his children. The keynote of his training and discipline was loving companionship. **Fond of Home**

He got down on the floor with them, took part in their play, invented all sorts of games for them, told them stories, wrote songs for them, narrated his adventures to them, kept up a perpetual undercurrent of moral and religious teaching, and impressed lessons of kindness, generosity, bravery, and truth.

His brother says of him : "The slightest appearance of selfishness or want of truth was severely dealt with, but when the rebuke was given there was an end of it, and he took pains to make the culprit feel that confidence was completely restored."

When he came home jaded and wounded from the battle he rested his great nature with an uproarious frolic with his children, who were always ready to impart of their superabundance of life to the wearied father or mother. What a power, what a galvanic battery a child is, to be sure.

He became the editor of the magazine called "Good Words," and in consequence the Philistines were upon him again, this time reinforced by the Pharisees. It was denounced by the leaders and organs of the Evangelical party in the

English Church, as though it had been edited by his satanic majesty himself. The word evangelical does not mean there what it means here. Here it refers to doctrines, whoever may hold them, there to one of the three parties—Ritualistic, Rationalistic, and Evangelical, or High, Broad, and Low; and the bitterest of these is the Low or Evangelical—bitterest toward the other two parties, bitterest toward the Nonconformists.

"Good Words" was banned and damned with all the authoritative ferocity with which the pope banishes heretical books to the Index Expurgatorius. The Free Church Assembly was overtured by one of the Presbyteries to look after this magazine. Here is a specimen attack:

"It was charged that a professor had publicly declared that he had read an article on astronomy in 'Good Words' on Sunday evening."

Dr. Macleod replied: "Why not take the magazine by the throat at 11.55 on Saturday night and incarcerate it till 12.05 Monday morning?"

The Philistines Again

"I was threatened that unless I gave up Stanley and Kingsley, I should be crushed." Dean Stanley and Charles Kingsley!

And this passage was quoted against the unholy alliance, "Thou shalt not plough with an ox and an ass together." But perhaps the kicking came of the fact that certain asses were not asked to help at the plowing.

The attack increased the sale of the magazine and the editor's determination to stand by it. He said: "The opposition gives frightful evidence of the low state to which pharisaical religion has come. I shall go on as I have begun, with a firm, clear purpose and a peaceful, courageous heart."

He said to the publisher: "Let us do what is right, and dare the devil, whether he comes as an infidel or a Pharisee."

So again the Lord delivered him out of the hands of the Philistines, and the rest of his days were days of prosperity and peace.

Nothing could better illustrate the difference between the atmosphere of this country and that of England than this preposterous opposition to this admirable magazine. It would not have happened in this country. There may be bigotry enough here, but it has no such party organization or narrow partisan motive. The intolerant in all denominations are restrained by the tolerant public opinion of the denomination to which they belong.

His sense of the ludicrous was of great use to him, as it is to any man who possesses it. It broke the force of many an attack. It acted as a buffer to the buffetings he was obliged to take from ignorance and bigotry. Hence the elasticity with which he met one of the most irrational and acrid gales of opposition that ever beat upon a brave and noble soul. No storms could sour his milk of human kindness.

His Sense of Humor

He was easily touched by such a story as this: "The grave-digger of Kilwinning parish was dying, and was questioned by his minister as to the cause of his sadness. The old grave-digger replied: 'Well, you

His Sense of Humor

see I was just thinking that I had buried fifty folk this year and I was hoping I might be spared to make out the hundred before the next new year.'"

He told me that once when an alarm of fire was raised in a great audience over which he was presiding he fell into a violent fit of laughter; and the people were quieted.

He was one of a club of literary satirists, the chief merit of whose productions was their absurdity. A toast having been proposed to poetry in rather disparaging terms, a poet responded in these words: "I will tell the gentlemen what poetry is. Poetry is the language of the tempest when it roars through the crashing forest. Poetry, sir, poetry was the voice which the Almighty thundered through the peaks of Sinai, and I myself, sir, have published five volumes of poetry, and the last, in its third edition, can be had for the price of five shillings and sixpence."

His jolly-heartedness enabled him to endure without discouragement and even to profit by the somewhat caustic criticism of the great organs of culture.

He wrote: "I am pretty well convinced from the reviews of 'Old Lieutenant' that I am not able to be of use in that line. The book is killed and buried forever, though self-love makes me think it cannot be so bad as they make it. I shall get what good I can out of the reviews."

Being so endowed with the sense of humor, we are not surprised to find that a corresponding sense of the pathetic went with it. He could sound the highest note of hilarious enjoyment and the lowest of pensive depression. These two experiences are inseparable and unavoidable. This is human nature. I have quoted from his sympathetic experiences at the time of the death of his brother. He abounded in sympathy and gentleness and humane pity.

Pathos and Humor

Furthermore, Dr. Macleod was an illustration of the equally well-established fact that such natures combine the keenest relish for the grotesque with the liveliest feeling of reverence. Some of the most reverent and spiritual men have been men of overflowing humor and fun. Dr. Macleod was a man of this sort. Consequently I am surprised that his biographer should express surprise at this.

He says: "Those who knew him only in society, buoyant and witty, overflowing with animal spirits, the very soul of laughter and enjoyment, may feel surprised at the almost morbid self-condemnation and excessive tenderness of conscience which his journals display, still more at the tone of sadness which so frequently pervades them. This tone of sadness must sound strange from one generally so buoyant."

This statement sounds strange, for if there is any fact respecting human nature or mental philosophy well established, it is that sadness is a constituent element of the buoyant nature.

Notice what he writes concerning his degree of D. D. received from Glasgow University:

"The University of Glasgow has this

Norman Macleod

day conferred upon me the degree of D. D. How sad it makes me! I feel as if it had stamped me with old age, and that it was a great cataract in the stream, leading more rapidly to the unfathomable gulf where all is still. . . . It needs all my faith to prevent my becoming peevish and miserable with myself."

He wrote: "Some will tell you that you deny the atonement unless you believe that Christ on the cross endured the punishment which was due to each sinner of the elect for whom he died, which thank God, I do not believe, as I know he died for the whole world."

His Theological Sentiments

"It is not enough to believe that sin is a curse, and that so long as a sinner remains in this world, or anywhere else, loving sin, he is in hell. You must believe in literal fire and brimstone, or you are not evangelical."

This reminds us of Finney:

"If Christ did not die for all men, how can it be said that God willeth all men to be saved? Or, how can all men be commanded to believe? What are they to believe? If it is said God knows that they will not come, this is charging God with conduct man would be ashamed of. If they may, but will not believe, this is moral guilt, not natural inability. . . A man must have hell taken out of himself before he can be said to be out of hell. . . Believing too much is more philosophical than believing nothing at all."

With a large experience of the one-man form of worship he preferred a more congenial form.

He said: "Our better-thinking clergy are beginning to see the use of a set form of worship. . . And who can look at the critical, self-sufficient faces of the one-half of our congregations during prayers, and the puffing and blowing of the minister, and not deplore the absence of some set prayers which would keep the feelings of many right-thinking Christians from being hurt every Sunday."

Again he said: "Neither money nor schools nor tracts can be substituted for living men. We want Christians, whether they be blacksmiths or shoemakers or lawyers, to remember their own responsibilities, and to be personal ministers for good."

A Living Man

This is what he was, a living man, a personal minister for good, a mighty man of valor, a splendid leader and captain in the camp of the King of saints, the Lord our Christ.

He died at the right time, in the right place, and in the right way. He died suddenly, which was his wish, and in the midst of his family, and at a time when his work seemed to be done and well done. He had fought a good fight; he had kept the faith.

His Death

He had won all the battles that had been given him to fight; his enemies were silenced. He had accomplished, or set in motion so that others could carry on, great and far-reaching measures for the enlightenment of the world, the rescue of the perishing, and the advancement of the church.

To be sure he was not very old, only

His Death

sixty, but old age is always within sight and near at hand to one of his temperament at that age. Some may hold their own after that for a time, but such are few. With the most of men of so rapid and intense a life the natural force is greatly abated at that age, and a quiet death is to be preferred to a dependent life. Happy the man who dies when his work is done.

While reclining on the sofa in great feebleness, he said: "All is perfect peace and perfect calm."

"I have glimpses of heaven that no pen or tongue or words can describe."

It was Sunday, and the bells had just ceased to ring, when his head fell back. There was a gentle sigh, and the great, brave heart of Norman Macleod ceased to beat for this world and began to beat for the other.

He slept with his fathers, and was buried with his fathers amid the glorious hills of his native land.

Such an ending of such a life is no place for discouragement and repining.

It is for reconsecrating ourselves to the Master whom he served so faithfully and whom we profess to serve. It is a place for that courage which he illustrated so admirably, and which rings in the verses he composed.

> Courage, brother, do not stumble,
>   Though thy path be dark as night
> There is a star to guide the humble,
>   Trust in God and do the right.
> Though the road be long and dreary,
>   And the end be out of sight;
> Foot it bravely, strong or weary,
>   Trust in God, and do the right.
>
> Perish policy and cunning,
>   Perish all that fears the light,
> Whether losing, whether winning,
>   Trust in God and do the right.
> Some will hate thee, some will love thee
>   Some will flatter, some will slight:
> Cease from man, and look above thee,
>   Trust in God and do the right.

CHARLES G. FINNEY

IV

CHARLES G. FINNEY was one of the most striking and unique religious forces of our times, the most remarkable revivalist this country has produced.

A Lawyer in the Pulpit

We shall study him from a human point of view and take for granted all that can be said of him from a divine point of view. We shall follow in the main his autobiography, a noteworthy book and worth your reading.

He was born in Warren, Conn., in 1792, and died in 1875, at eighty-three years of age. He enjoyed the privileges of a common school until he was fifteen years of age, and became a school-teacher himself.

A Revivalist with Intellect

Here is another of the powerful men who may be said to be the growth of our common school system.

He thought of going to Yale College,

but his preceptor, who was a graduate of Yale, dissuaded him, saying it would be a loss of time, as he could accomplish the curriculum in two years instead of four, as required by the college. He says, "I acquired some knowledge of Latin, Greek, and Hebrew, but I was never a classical scholar." But he was a scholar in the English language. He was an educated man in the best sense of the phrase, well furnished for the work for which he was adapted. The end of all education is to know what to do, and how to do it. He knew how to make the most of himself.

He selected the law as his profession, but was soon converted and left it for the ministry. This was at twenty-six years of age.

His experience at conversion is a revelation of the man; his temperament, his emotional nature, his depth of sensibility. "The rising of my soul was so great that I rushed into the back room of the law office to pray, when it seemed as if I met the Lord Jesus face to face. It did not occur to me then,"—this is a character-

A Revivalist with Intellect

istic description,—"nor for some time afterward, that this was wholly a mental state. On the contrary, it seemed to me that I saw him as I would see any other man. I wept aloud like a child. It seemed to me that I bathed his feet with my tears. I literally bellowed out the unutterable gushings of my heart." An elder of the church came in and asked him how he felt, and when he learned, the elder fell into a spasmodic fit of laughter. This illustrates the great diversity and contrariety of forms in religious experience; what is one man's meat is another man's—laughing-stock.

We see that he was a man of great religious sensibility, of an unusual emotional development, with a tendency to take account and make account of his emotional experiences. In the course of his autobiography, we are told of the ineffable light that shone into his soul, almost prostrating him to the ground.

"The Lord drew so near to me while I was engaged in prayer, that my flesh literally trembled on my bones. It seemed more like being on the top of Sinai, amidst its thunderings, than in the presence of the cross of Christ."

Here you have a foretaste of remarkable expression, language, utterance, and rhetoric, the power of figurative expression which has distinguished all great preachers, and without which there can be no effective preaching.

He resolved to prepare for the ministry. Deacon B. came into the office and said to him:

"Mr. Finney, do you recollect that my cause is to be tried at ten o'clock this morning? I suppose you are ready."

Finney replied: "Deacon, I have a retainer from the Lord Jesus to plead his cause and I cannot plead yours."

The deacon looked at him in astonishment and asked: "What do you mean?"

Finney replied that he had enlisted in the cause of Christ, and that he had a retainer from the Lord Jesus to plead his cause. Some lawyers behave as though they had a retainer from a very different person.

A Revivalist with Intellect

Some graduates of Princeton Theological Seminary tried to persuade him to study there, but he refused, saying he would not put himself under such influence as they had been under. They had been wrongly educated, and did not meet his ideal of what a minister of Christ should be.

He commenced his studies under his pastor, and began then and there to apply his splendid logical faculty and controversial acuteness to the prevailing form of doctrinal preaching, which was freezing the water of everlasting life, so that however free and refreshing it may be as it bursts from its fountain on the New Testament page, it becomes as it flows from the lips of the preacher—an icicle. Finney's pastor and teacher was one of this school of theologians and preachers, and Finney was not. So the young man set about knocking the nonsense out of the old man's head.

His teacher held that the human constitution was morally depraved, that men were utterly unable to comply with the terms of the gospel, to repent or to believe, or to do anything that God required them to do; that while they were free to do all evil, in the sense of being able to commit any amount of sin, yet they were not free to perform any good; that God condemned them for their sinful nature, and for this as well as for their transgressions they deserved eternal death.

He told his pastor he took it for granted that his hearers were theologians, and that he assumed many things which needed to be proved. This did not suit Finney and he said so. It may not suit some who do not say so.

You see then the cast and make of this man's mind; it required proof, evidence, clearness, candor, honesty, in the preacher as well as the politician.

Finney repudiated and combatted at once these doctrines, to the great dismay of his teacher, who "warned him that if he would persist in reasoning on these subjects instead of receiving them, he would land in infidelity."

At his examination by the presbytery

he was asked if he received the Confession of Faith. He says:

"I had not examined it, that is, the large work containing the catechism and confession. This had made no part of my study. I replied that I received it for substance of doctrine, so far as I understood it. But I spoke in a way that plainly implied, I think, that I did not pretend to know much about it. When I came to read the Confession of Faith and ponder it, I saw that although I could receive it, as I know multitudes do, as containing the substance of Christian doctrine, yet there were several points upon which I could not put the same construction that was put on them at Princeton; and I accordingly, everywhere, gave the people to understand that I did not accept that construction; or if that was the true construction, then I entirely differed from the Confession of Faith."

He was struck with the fact that the prayers he heard at prayer meetings were not answered, and that those who offered them did not regard them as answered;

they had not the faith to expect God to give them what they asked for. He says again:

"On one occasion, when I was in one of the prayer meetings, I was asked if I did not desire that they should pray for me. I told them no; because I did not see that God answered their prayers. I said: 'I suppose I need to be prayed for, I am conscious that I am a sinner; but I do not see that it will do any good for you to pray for me, for you are continually asking, but you do not receive. You have been praying for the Holy Spirit to descend upon yourselves, and yet complaining of your leanness. You have prayed enough since I have attended these meetings to have prayed the devil out of Adams, if there is any virtue in your prayers. But here you are praying on, and complaining still.'"

<small>Praying and Complaining</small>

There is a great deal of complaining that tries to pass for praying. Some of us act as though we were commanded to complain without ceasing.

We find him beginning to preach, and we find that he began as he continued and ended, a lawyer, resolved to have a verdict on the spot or know the reason why.

He exclaims: "I talked to the people as I would have talked to a jury. Of all the causes that were ever plead, the cause of religion, I thought, had the fewest able advocates, and that if advocates at the bar should pursue the same course in pleading the cause of their clients that ministers do in pleading the cause of Christ with sinners, they would not gain a single case."

His fellow-ministers complained not only of what he preached but of how he preached it. Of them he writes: "I used to meet from ministers a great many rebuffs and reproofs in respect to my manner of preaching." They reproved him for illustrating his ideas by reference to the common affairs of men of different occupations.

They would say: "Why do you not illustrate from events of ancient history, and take a more dignified way of illustrating your ideas?"

To this he replied: "If my illustrations were new and striking they would occupy the minds of the hearers instead of the truth which I wished to illustrate."

He began by being ornate, but became direct and simple in style. When he came to preach the gospel he says he was so anxious to be thoroughly understood that he "studied on the one hand to avoid what was vulgar, and on the other to express my thoughts with the greatest simplicity of language."

He took a commission from a ladies' missionary society, and this mighty man of God began his preaching at Evans Mills, New York State. The people thronged the place and extolled his preaching. But so far from being pleased and inflated by their flattery, he was offended by it and resented it. He rolled it as a sweet morsel under his—feet.

What he wanted was a verdict for his client. He told them that something was wrong in him or in them, that the kind

A Law of Rhetoric

of interest they manifested in his preaching was doing them no good, and that he could not spend his time with them unless they were going to receive the gospel.

He requested those who were willing to make their peace with God to rise up, and those who were unwilling to sit still. They looked at one another and all sat still, as he had expected. They began to look angry and arose and started for the door. He paused, and they paused, and he said he was sorry for them and would preach to them once more the next night.

They all left the house, except a deacon, who came up to him and said:

"Brother Finney, you have got them. They cannot rest under this, rely upon it. The brethren are all discouraged, but I am not. I believe you have done the very thing that needed to be done, and that we shall see the results."

The deacon and Mr. Finney went into the grove together and spent the afternoon in prayer, while the people were threatening to give the revivalist a coat of tar and feathers and ride him on a rail. The evening came, and with it a crowd far greater than could get into the schoolhouse. He says: "For more than an hour the word of God came through me to them in a manner that I could see was carrying all before it. Many of them could not hold up their heads." This was the beginning of the physical or mental effects of his preaching. A woman fell down speechless, and was carried from the house in a kind of trance. A man who had sworn that he would kill Finney and had brought a pistol to the meeting fell from his seat and shrieked that he was sinking to hell. He was soon delivered and in ecstasy. Men of the strongest nerves were so cut down that they had to be carried home by their friends. This he should not have allowed. The fact that Moody has nothing of this proves that there need be nothing of it.

He could control the physical excitement as well as arouse it. He was mighty in command. On one occasion when he saw that there was danger of an uproar,

A Man with a Will of his Own

he says he told the people to kneel down and to keep so quiet that they could hear every word of his prayer. They did so and the excitement subsided. His prayer was adroitly fashioned for the occasion.

His will power was tremendous and is worthy of study from the point of view of mental philosophy, as well as from that of practical preaching. Bear in mind that we are looking at him from the human side, and take for granted all that can be said and all that he says on the divine or supernatural side.

We observe the exercise of this will power upon himself, for he commanded himself as well as other people.

He was one of those men who never say die or even cry sick, and who defy the doctors to prove that they are going to die. The physicians told him that he had the consumption—and he had. They told him that he would never labor any more in revivals, but he labored a whole lifetime in revivals after that. They told him that he could live but a little while, but he lived about fifty years after they said so. He told the doctors of bodies just what he told the doctors of souls, that they were mistaken; and they were.

He coughed blood when he was licensed, and his friends thought he could live but a short time. He was charged not to preach more than once a week and not more than half an hour at a time; all of which he proceeded not to do.

He plunged head-foremost and heart-foremost into a preaching campaign of six months' duration.

He says: "I preached out of doors. I preached in barns. I preached in schoolhouses. I preached nearly every night. I preached about two hours at a time. Before the six months were completed my health was entirely restored, my lungs were sound, and a glorious revival spread all over that region of country."

If you spend all your time in nursing yourself, you will never be anything but a nurse. Vanity is at the bottom of our coddling ourselves. We pretend that we are saving ourselves for the Lord's work,

His Preaching an Assault upon the Will

when we would save ourselves much more successfully if we would do as Finney did, throw ourselves into that work. But suppose you die? Die then. "He that saveth his life shall lose it, and he that loseth his life for my sake, shall find it." This Finney pluck and will is the stuff to make preachers out of, or any other man out of, who has to earn his bread by as much sweat of the brow as is distilled out of him by this climate.

It is curious and instructive to note that Finney being a man of great will-power himself, appealed perpetually to that power in his hearers. He compelled them to come in and to give in. It was a conflict of wills in this conflict between preacher and hearer, and there were few wills that could stand against one so self-reliant and aggressive as that of Charles G. Finney.

Here is his keynote idea: the command to obey implies the ability to obey him; a man's "cannot" is his will-not, and his "will" is his can.

He says: "I assumed that moral depravity is and must be a voluntary attitude of the mind, that it does and must consist in the committal of the will to the gratification of the desires.

"One doctor of divinity told me that he felt a great deal more like weeping over sinners than blaming them.

"I replied that I did not wonder, if he believed that they had a sinful nature, and that sin was entailed upon them and they could not help it."

He declared that it was putting a stumblingblock in the way of the church and the world to teach, "A nature sinful in itself, a total inability to obey God, and condemnation to eternal death for the sin of Adam. When men asked God to forgive them, they were to commit themselves unalterably to his will."

"Nothing was in the way of their offering acceptable prayer but their own obstinacy."

"It was plain," he says of one place, "that nothing could be done unless the pastor's views could be changed." So with the pastor in the pulpit behind him and the congregation before him, Finney opened his battery on front and rear. He says he "endeavored to show that if man was as helpless as their views represented him to be, he was not to blame for his sins. If he had lost in Adam all power of obedience, so that obedience had become impossible to him, it was mere nonsense to say that he could be blamed for what he could not help.

"Some looked distressed, others offended; some laughed, some wept, and the pastor moved himself from one end of the sofa to the other, in the pulpit behind me, breathing and sighing audibly. When I was through I did not invite the pastor to pray, for I dared not, but prayed myself that the Lord would set home the word."

Wary man! He was quite right, and quite like a lawyer who does not propose to allow his opponent the last word with judge or jury if he can help it.

As they were passing out, a lady said to her pastor: "If that sermon be the truth, you have never preached the gospel;" and the pastor replied, "I am sorry to say I never have."

Once in England he listened to a sermon in which repentance was represented not as a voluntary, but as an involuntary change, and consisting of a mere state of sensibility, and the impenitent were told to go home and pray for repentance. Finney says he "found it difficult to keep from screaming to the people to repent, and not to think they were doing their duty in merely praying for repentance."

Repentance not a Dogma but a Conduct

It seems to me that John the Baptist would have felt the same impulse and in all probability would have acted upon it.

Here again he was logical. He held that the religion of the New Testament is a total abstinence from anything and anybody that simply amuses or pleases, and that every word of instruction to the first twelve Christians is binding upon every one of the present twelve millions, more or less, of Christians.

Repentance not a Dogma but a Conduct

Your only escape from that logic is just one other, and the only other logic: the rules for the government of the individual are left to the inward light of that individual, whether it be for croquet, cards, dancing, or the preaching of women.

A man of strong will, high character, and prominent position, rebelled against the favorite idea of Finney, that "the sinner's cannot is his will not." This Mr. H—— insisted that this was false in his case, that he was willing to be a Christian.

"I did not spare him," says Mr. Finney, "but from day to day I hunted him from his refuges, and answered all his objections and met all his excuses."

The man was driven to prayer, and commenced with the Lord's Prayer, but when he came to "Thy will be done," he was brought face to face with the will of God, and found that what Finney had told him was true; he was not willing that God's will should be done. He gathered up all his strength of will and cried aloud, "Thy will be done on earth as it is in heaven," and was "perfectly conscious that his will went with the words."

On one occasion after the choir had executed an anthem so scientifically that not a word was distinguishable, Mr. Finney prayed: "Lord, we trust thou hast understood the song that thy servants have tried to sing. Thou knowest that we could not understand a word of it."

It was in a "burnt district," or a section where there had been an extravagant religious excitement, with the usual mischievous reaction.

A Humdrum Prayer Meeting

"I found that it had left among Christian people some practices that were offensive, and calculated rather to excite ridicule than any serious conviction of the truth of religion. For example, in all their prayer meetings I found a custom prevailing like this: every professor of religion felt it a duty to testify for Christ. They must take up the cross and say something in meeting. One would rise and say in substance: 'I have a duty to perform which no one can perform for

A Humdrum Prayer Meeting

me. I arise to testify that religion is good; though I must confess that I do not enjoy it at present. I have nothing in particular to say, only to bear my testimony; and I hope you will all pray for me.' This concluded, that person would sit down and another would rise and say, 'Religion is good; I do not enjoy it; I have nothing else to say, but I must do my duty. I hope you will all pray for me.' Of course the ungodly would make sport of this; it was in fact ridiculous and repulsive."

To counteract the effect of this he substituted preaching services interspersed with prayers. He would talk awhile, and call upon some sensible brother to pray awhile, and then he would resume his discourse.

He was abundant in explicit and persistent prayer. He writes, at one time: "I saw no means of providing for my family through the winter. Thanksgiving Day came, and found us so poor that I had been obliged to sell my traveling trunk, which I had used in my evangelistic labors, to supply the place of a cow which I had lost. I rose on the morning of Thanksgiving, and spread our necessities before the Lord. I finally concluded by saying that if help did not come, I should assume that it was best that it should not, and would be entirely satisfied with any course that the Lord would see it wise to take."

He returned home after preaching, to find a check for two hundred dollars from Mr. Josiah Chapin, of Providence, who continued to send him six hundred a year for several years, and on this he managed to live.

Rich men should answer the prayers of poor men, especially if the poor man should happen to be a preacher. It is strange that it does not occur to rich Christians that if they are unable to preach or teach themselves they can pay the salaries of those who are trying to preach in spite of the poverty that breaks their hearts, ruins their health, and shortens their lives. Rich Christians can endow chairs of Christian usefulness.

His Method with Skeptics

He was wont to say: "If a right course is taken with skeptics, they can be shut up to condemnation by their own irresistible convictions, and they will rejoice to find a door of mercy opened to them."

Here is his method with an inquiring theist. The man said, in reply to a question, that he believed in the existence of God, and that he ought to worship and obey him but did not.

"Well, then," exclaimed Mr. Finney, "why should I give you further information and further light, if you will not do your duty and obey the light you already have? When you will make up your mind to live up to your convictions, to obey God according to the best light you have; when you will make up your mind to repent of your neglect thus far, and to please God just as well as you know how, the rest of your life, I will try to show you that the Bible is from God. Until then it is of no use to do any such thing."

The man admitted that that was fair, went away, did as he was directed, and became a Christian, a trustee of Oberlin, and an influential and generous man.

While there was a general uniformity in the method of his preaching, he was as flexible as adroit in preaching for special cases. *Wise to Win Souls* A good woman and devoted Christian got into a despairing frame of mind, and yet was expressing her concern for an impenitent young man who violently opposed the revival. Mr. Finney said to her:

"Aunt Lucy, when you and B. die God will have to make a partition in hell and give you a room by yourself."

"Oh, Mr. Finney!"

"Yes," replied Mr. Finney. "Here he is raving against God, and here you are almost insane to see him in this condition. Can two persons in two such opposite frames of mind, do you think, be sent to the same place?"

Her features relaxed, and she smiled for the first time in many days. Finally she laughed and said, "We cannot." Her despair cleared up and she was as happy as a young convert.

He was good at getting people out of the theological dilemmas in which they had become involved by an erroneous education. A thoughtful man told him that he could not receive the Bible because it teaches that "God has imputed Adam's sin to all his posterity, that we inherit the guilt of that sin by nature, and are exposed to eternal damnation for the guilt of Adam's sin."

Finney asked him for the chapter and verse, and the man quoted the catechism, and that was all he knew of the Bible, and he thought that that was all Finney knew of the Bible; but he was mistaken. Finney then gave him what he believed the Bible taught about Adam's sin and his own—reasoned with him of these things—and the man was enlightened, satisfied, and converted.

Of this incident he says, "I felt it my duty to expose all the hiding-places of sinners and to hunt them out from under those peculiar views of orthodoxy in which I found them entrenched."

He hunted them out from under the

delusion that man ought to be willing to be damned for the glory of God. He knocked that nonsense out of them. Happy is the preacher who has the art of knocking the nonsense out of people without knocking their heads off.

Nothing demonstrates so clearly the reality of conversion as a change of disposition. The vicious became virtuous, the penurious generous, the selfish self-sacrificing. *Financial Conversions* He compelled sinners to confess not the sins of Adam, but their own, according to the Scriptures. Under his preaching criminals confessed, not simply their abstract or theoretical sinfulness, but their actual crimes. Both in England and this country, numerous and large amounts of money were refunded by persons who had stolen them, or obtained them through meanness or deception. Business men of good repute came forward and acknowledged their sins of overreaching their customers, or underpaying their clerks, or undermining their competitors.

Financial Conversions

While he was expounding the Golden Rule, a man arose and asked if a certain case came under his interpretation of the rule. Mr. Finney said it would. The man went away and made restitution of thirty thousand dollars.

At one of his revival meetings a man was observed forcing a companion into the house and to the front seat. The coerced hearer was found to be utterly indifferent, and the man who compelled him to come was asked for an explanation. He said he observed that Mr. Finney's preaching made men conscientious and induced them to pay their debts. Several of Finney's converts had paid him debts that were outlawed. "This fellow owes me several hundred dollars, and I thought if he could only be converted under Mr. Finney I could get my pay."

He insisted upon religion and not alone upon the subject of religion, and was himself driven by a religious motive and not simply by a partiality for the subject of religion. Crooked saints were straightened out, and the croakers ceased to croak and began to find something in the sermon to enjoy besides its defects. An old lady used to bore the women's meetings with her long and tedious whine. She had the impression that it was her duty to speak at every meeting; and sometimes she would get up and complain of the Lord, that he made it her duty to speak, while the fine ladies who could speak so much to edification, were allowed to attend and "have no cross," as she expressed it, "to take up." A new spirit came upon her; a great change came over her. She ceased to complain and spoke to edification. Everybody was interested and she became a great favorite.

His interest in lawyers, and their interest in his preaching, illustrate his partiality for appealing to the reason and the understanding, rather than the emotions. He says, "I was particularly interested in lawyers. I knew they were more controlled by argument, evidence, and logical statements than any other

Good for the Hard=headed

class." Many lawyers and judges were among his converts.

Physicians he found more difficult. "I think their studies incline them to skepticism and a certain form of materialism."

Lawyer: A theory comes first and is indispensable. Physician: A theory comes last, or never, since it is never indispensable. So a lawyer's Christianity might be more insincere and fallacious than a physician's agnosticism.

He was a preacher of the gospel after the manner of the revivalists without degenerating into an auctioneer of the gospel. He did not fall into the professional, "Going—going—gone!" style of dealing out the good news of eternal life. He did not make converts in order to count them, he made converts that could be counted upon. There are no spiritual statistics in his book; no figuring up of converts that the Lord had enabled him to count.

He did not undertake to convert souls

by simply raising the temperature of the body, turning them into a small room and turning on the gas, and the heat, and the rhetoric, and the morbid tears of a heavy supper and Japanese tea. He used no incubator.

The longer he lived the narrower he became with respect to the human animal's need of amusement.

The Victim of his own Logic He even by a droll twist of thought called religion an amusement. The highest amusement is found in doing the will of God. How easy to prove then that the self-denial which he insists upon as indispensable to Christianity becomes self-indulgence.

Great logicians fail in logic, as all the strong characters fail in what they are great in.

With all his gift of logic he would resort to this trick of the rhetorician. This god on the intellectual Olympus would come down among the cheap preachers who quarrel with the new and true version because it substitutes the awful fact of condemnation for the more rhetorical of damnation. "Shalt be condemned!" that is logic which carries the reason. "Shalt be damned!" that is crying "Boo," which startles the nerves, weak nerves.

You will find in his autobiography no elaborate or detailed history of his revivals in Rochester, Philadelphia, Boston, or England, but they are touched upon with a sententious force and comprehensive skill that cannot but fascinate as well as tantalize.

His connection with the college at Oberlin does not occupy much of his memoir, and must be omitted from this address; but it should be elaborated in a full history of Finney's work. Whether considered educationally, politically, theologically, or religiously, it is a period of marked importance.

He was ordained a Presbyterian and became a Congregationalist, but he stood apart and worked apart from all denominations, owing to the attitude of the churches toward slavery and toward the education of the colored people. He was a Christian unattached.

Among his obstacles were ill-constructed audience rooms, obstacles which that arch-architect, the arch-adversary, delights to put into the way of the gospel. So he planned one to suit himself, the Broadway Tabernacle, New York.

He says: " The plan of the interior of that house was my own. I had observed the defects of churches in regard to sound, and was sure that I could give the plan of a church in which I could easily speak to a much larger congregation than any house would hold that I had ever seen. An architect was consulted, and I gave him my plan. But he objected to it, that it would not appear well, and feared that it would injure his reputation to build a church with such an interior as that. I told him that if he would not build it on that plan, he was not the man to superintend its construction at all. It was finally built in accordance with my ideas; and it was a most commodious and comfortable place to speak in."

Opposition

They gave him his "vinegar to drink." He was opposed in such a manner and in such a variety of forms, and by such a variety and diversity of people, with so much virulence and vehemence, as to bring to mind, as no other page of modern ecclesiastical history does, the opposition which Christianity met with in the days of its Founder. Piety and impiety, orthodoxy and heterodoxy, Calvinist and rationalist, Pilate and Herod, joined hands against him.

He was opposed by Presbyterians, old school, new school, and no school, by Methodists, Baptists, Congregationalists, Universalists, Unitarians, Deists, Theists, and Atheists, by Princeton, and Andover, and Harvard, and Yale, by all the "schools" and all the fools, by D. D.'s and LL. D.'s. They found fault with his doctrine, his rhetoric, with everything he did and the method by which he did it.

The Rev. Mr. Patterson, a Presbyterian minister of Philadelphia, said to him when he came there: "If the Presbyterian ministers find out your views, they will hunt you out of the city as they would a wolf."

Finney replied very much after the manner of one of Luther's replies: "I can preach no other doctrine. I do not believe that they can get me out of Philadelphia."

Some held their garments away from him. He invited an old lady to ride with him as she seemed unable to walk. When she was seated she asked who he was, and where he lived, and upon being told, replied: "Oberlin! Why, our minister said he would just as soon send a son to State prison as to Oberlin."

An eminent Doctor of Divinity says that he said to Mr. Finney: "Finney, I know your plan and you know I do; you mean to come to Connecticut, and carry a streak of fire to Boston. But if you attempt it, as the Lord liveth, I'll meet you at the State line, and call out all the artillerymen, and fight every inch of the way to Boston, and then I'll fight you there."

He was pursued and persecuted for

Opposition

preaching what Mr. Moody now preaches on a platform covered with the clergy of all denominations, what the Methodist preachers have always preached, and what is heard now from nine hundred and ninety-nine out of every thousand Congregationalist and Baptist pulpits, and from almost as large a proportion of Presbyterian pulpits.

He was tried by newspaper, by Presbytery, by committee; and a great convention sat upon him—without crushing him. The abjects gathered themselves together against him. He was denounced as a lunatic, a fanatic, a madman, an amalgamationist, a heretic, an Arminian, and an abolitionist.

He was accused of conspiring to unite Church and State. He was assailed by the daily paper, by the weekly paper, and by the quarterly review. He was arraigned in book form and pamphlet form, and in a form of godliness without the power thereof, in private letters and public letters signed by distinguished and extinguished names and no names at all.

He was dogged in this country and went to England only to find that leading men had written and spoken against his views without having read a line of them, except as they came from his enemies. He was followed and preceded by spies. His meetings were caricatured and his preaching travestied. His methods were misrepresented and his motives maligned. False witnesses did rise up and laid to his charge things that he knew not. "They rewarded me evil for good to the spoiling of my soul."

In short he was pursued by all manner of vilification, calumny, and slander, except that of a moral nature. Not a breath was ever breathed so far as I can learn, against his moral character, social or financial. There was no financial scandal connected with his meetings; he did not beg for money, or for letters from converts. He was poor in everything except good works and—a good wife.

He was rich only in faith—but so rich in that, that he was fed by rich saints, which is more than can be said of Elijah,

As a Moral Force

and quenched his thirst by smiting the rock of penurious religion, which is more than can be said of Moses, and much more than can be said of thousands of preachers who have to turn away in despair from their hard-hearted, well-to-do parishioners, and get their food from the ravens and their water from the rock, or not at all ; and all the people say, Amen.

Considered exclusively as a moral force, manifested in changing the characters upon which he brought himself to bear, he is one of the most unique and commanding men of modern times.

As a study in character he will reward the student of human nature abundantly, in any one of the marked and striking phases which he represents. He will yield wonderful results whether as a religious force or as a moral force or as an intellectual force ; whether as a leader of thought, or as a theologian, or as a religious reformer.

He reminds one of the Apostle Paul in emotional intensity, in hard-headedness, in vigor of understanding, in logical acumen, in unremitting zeal, in pressing for immediate results, in forcing a verdict on the spot, in will and in assaulting the will, in passionate tenacity of purpose, and in exclusive self-denying devotion to Jesus Christ.

One half a century he spent in the service of God and of man, of heaven and of earth, of religion and of morals, of the Christian religion and the public welfare.

I should say that he was a fanatic in the sense that Luther was, and Knox, and Calvin, and Arminius, and Savonarola. He ran out at some points in an excessive manner. He was narrow at the top in comparison with his base. He was a fanatic in the sense that all agitators are fanatical, whether political or religious, whether anti-slavery, or anti-intemperance, anti-religious-torpor, or anti-anything else. It is impossible for such forces to get on, or do much without doing too much, to do anything without overdoing it. But what man of this great century can

Was He a Fanatic?

And He Died Also

show a grander or sublimer record? Who can measure his influence for righteousness, its breadth, its depth, its duration?

The many contrivances, or devices, or machinery shown at the Centennial Exhibition were interesting and wonderful, but there was no such power of engineering or forces on exhibition as this man was. Their use will end and their influence perish; his influence will endure through all time and all eternity. The men of the century are imperishable.

That one event which happeneth unto all happened unto him. His last day on earth was a quiet Sunday, August 16, 1875. He was within two weeks of his eighty-third birthday. He walked out with his wife at sunset and listened to the music in the church near by. He returned and joined with his family in singing "Jesus Lover of my Soul." During the night he was seized with pains at the heart and began to sink. About two o'clock in the morning he asked for some water. But it could not quench his thirst, and he said, "Perhaps this is the thirst of death." A moment afterward he added, "I am dying," and he died.

The lesson he would have us learn from his dying words is the same that he would have us learn from him as a living epistle for fifty years: If any man have the thirst of death, he can have the "Water of Life," if he will.

> Jesus, lover of my soul
>   Let me to thy bosom fly,
> While the raging billows roll,
>   While the tempest still is high.
> Hide me, O my Saviour, hide,
>   Till the storm of life is past,
> Safe into the haven guide
>   O receive my soul at last.

HUGH LATIMER

V

HUGH LATIMER was born at Thurcaston, Leicestershire, England, in 1490, seven years after Luther.

His father was a well-to-do farmer, or renter, and rented enough land to keep half a dozen men employed. He kept one hundred sheep and Mrs. Latimer milked thirty cows and brought up seven children in godliness and the fear of the Lord. His father made enough to give Hugh a university education, and to give his sisters five pounds and twenty nobles apiece as their marriage portion. His father was a soldier as well as a farmer, a sort of citizen soldier, always ready to get down his bow and arrows in defense of king and country.

Birth and Parentage

In the first picture we have of the boy Hugh, he is helping his father to buckle on his armor, for he is going to help Henry

Hugh Latimer

VII. put down the Cornish rebels at Blackheath Field. We have no details of his early history, or for that matter of any of his history. He had a godly bringing up, and was trained in the honesty and integrity which he afterward preached.

His Early History

At fourteen years of age he entered the University of Cambridge, the same year that Luther entered the University of Erfurt. The sixteenth century brought in with it some men that make it memorable and illustrious: Luther, Knox, Calvin, Ridley, Cranmer, Latimer, and Tyndale. He received his degree of Master of Arts at twenty-four years of age.

He studied divinity and began to preach. His preaching roused Cambridge. It was rousing preaching, caustic, witty, daring, for he was a born preacher. He preached against wickedness, but he was a Roman Catholic, zealous and bitter against the Reformers. He says he was as obstinate a Papist as there was in England. His oration at his taking of his Bachelor of

His Early History

Divinity degree was an answer to Melancthon, Luther's right-hand man.

One writer says of him: "He held the Reformers in such horror that he thought they were the supporters of Anti-Christ, whose appearance was to precede the coming of the Son of Man, and conjectured that the day of judgment was at hand." To his mind every commotion was the coming of the day of judgment. He used his wit and ridicule upon a fellow-student, Stafford, who had adopted the reform opinions, but a fellow-preacher, Thomas Bilney, used his powers of persuasion on him and his eyes were opened by Bilney. Great epochs in the lives of individuals and of nations are brought about by the influence of one man over another. One man converts another. The words of the wise are as nails. Death and life are in the power of the tongue. Latimer says, "He called me to knowledge."

He joined the Reformers and his preaching was a trumpet call to a life consistent with the profession of the Christian religion. It was a direct, open, personal assault upon the vices of individuals in his congregation. He withstood to the face the ecclesiastics, priests, and preachers, who were to be blamed for neglecting their duties. He was terribly vehement in his rebukes of the idle and vicious in high places. He denounced preachers and bishops for "stuffing themselves like the hogs of Epicure's flock, taking no thought though their poor parishioners miserably pine away and die of hunger."

He Joins the Reformers

Protestantism has always been and continues to be a struggle out from under the incubus of superstition and priestcraft.

The effect of his preaching was instantaneous and profound. One of his hearers says his sermons left pricks and stings in the hearts of his hearers which moved them to conform their lives to his preaching. Some went to hear him preach, "swelling, blown-full, and puffed up like Esop's frog" with envy and malice against him, but when they were asked how they liked the preaching they an-

He Joins the Reformers

swered, "Never man spake like this man."

"None but the stiff-necked and uncircumcised in heart went away from his sermons without being affected with high detestation of sin, and moved to all godliness and virtue."

One of the stiff-necked who went away from his preaching with a high detestation of Latimer instead of his own sin, was the bishop of Ely.

While Latimer was preaching the bishop came into the church with a lot of priests at his heels. Latimer paused until his lordship was seated.

Perhaps the bishop and perhaps the audience thought it was a mark of deference on the part of the preacher. If so, they were mistaken. The preacher had no deference for men of high station if they were men of low morals. Especially did he detest the sin of high ecclesiastics, who attempted to cover their rascalities with the regimentals of the church.

So when the Bishop of Ely had taken his seat, Latimer dropped the subject he had in hand, and took another—took the bishop for a subject. He proceeded to take the likeness of a model bishop, one that feared God and loved righteousness. His lordship of Ely knew so well that it was not his likeness that he was offended at it. He knew that was what a bishop ought to be and that he was not what he ought to be. His lordship ran to his cardinal after his thrashing like a whipped schoolboy to his mamma. The cardinal listened to the bishop's complaint that Preacher Latimer had hit him with a sermon, and sent for the preacher and asked him what he had said that gave his lordship of Ely so much offense.

The cardinal, so far from being displeased was delighted, and said to Latimer: "If the Bishop of Ely cannot abide such doctrine as you have here repeated you shall preach it to his beard, let him say what he will." The bishop forbade him to preach in his diocese, but the cardinal gave him a license to preach in any church in England.

In this cardinal we have come upon the

name of Wolsey, the renowned Cardinal Wolsey. You see what an era of history we are in, of history and historical characters, both royal and ecclesiastical. One of the most conspicuous characters of history and of Shakespeare is Wolsey, Henry VIII.'s crafty, ambitious, unscrupulous, and powerful minister, whose high-blown pride finally broke under him, and who died of a broken heart saying, "If I had served my God as diligently as I have served my king, he would not have forsaken me in mine age." Wolsey too seemed to have a liking for the plucky preacher. Something in him won the cardinal, who was ambitious to be pope. It was this preaching of righteousness to the beards of the unrighteous that made Latimer obnoxious to the world, the flesh, and the church.

We have no account of his domestic life—he had none; but he was abundant in domestic virtues and kindly graces. He was kind to the poor, sympathetic toward the unfortunate, full of alms-deeds.

Hugh Latimer

His parish life was his home life and his parishoners were his children. He practised what he preached, goodness, brotherly love, honesty, and went about doing good.

The Bible was published into Latin, and the ecclesiastical authorities kept tight hold of what few copies there were. Latimer advocated its publication in English, the language of the people. A friar answered him by saying that if the people were allowed to read the Bible, "the farmer would stop plowing lest he should peradventure disobey the Scripture, by looking back after he had put his hand to the plow, and the baker would be afraid to leaven his bread lest a little leaven should leaven the whole lump."

Humor was one of the elements of his power as a preacher; it feathered the arrow. He had an alert sense of the ludicrous and it gave him elasticity. Instead of breaking he would bend under the storm that beat upon him.

Henry VIII., of unsavory memory, was king of England. What recollections at

Henry VIII. was king of England

the mention of his name! The king who married his third wife the next day after beheading his second, and took off the head of his fifth wife in the height of their honeymoon! He liked Latimer; the corrupt monarch befriended the godly preacher. In 1530 he made him his chaplain. It was a strange alliance and was to have a strange effect upon the cause of the Reformation. Drawn together in person they parted company at once and forever with respect to the Reformed Faith.

While Latimer was answering Melancthon, Henry was answering Luther. But Latimer broke off there and pronounced unequivocally for the Protestant movement. Henry continued to stand between the pope and his opponents, and to play fast and loose with the Protestants and the pope to the end. So far as he became their friend he was impelled by the worst of motives.

The king's meanness promoted Protestantism. On December 1, 1530, he re-

Hugh Latimer

ceived a benediction from the pope as a reward for his opposition to Luther. The pope called him "Defender of the Faith."

Will the chaplaincy silence Latimer? Was it given for that purpose? "Ye seek me, not because ye saw the miracle, but because ye did eat of the loaves and were filled."

No, Latimer was not the man to sell his birthright of free speech for an office. He wrote his master a letter. It had a ring of fine mettle in it. He told the king to be a faithful minister of God's gifts, and not a defender of his faith. "For God will not have his cause defended by man or man's power. . . Wherefore remember that the day is at hand when you shall give account of the blood that hath been spilt by your sword." This was bold talk.

Latimer used his position for shielding the Protestants from the devouring rage of their enemies, but he did not accomplish much. Henry forbade the circulation or reading of Tyndale's English Bible, and Latimer wrote the king a letter of remonstrances, to which Henry paid no attention.

Never was a game of chess played with living men more complex or perplexing. On one side of the board was a bad pope, and on the other side of the board was a worse king. Their moves, from the worst of motives, affected the best of causes. Reformation was promoted or retarded by the wicked whims of powerful men thrown into power by the accident of birth. Righteousness and liberty were in the keeping of crowned villainy.

Latimer became participant in an influential event. In 1530 he became one of the commission that sat upon the divorce of Henry VIII. from Catharine of Aragon. He approved that scandalous act, and preached before the king on the following Sunday, and the king, we are told, greatly praised the sermon.

Henry was excommunicated by the pope for his divorce from Catharine and became head of the Church of England.

Wolsey's intrigue with the pope in favor of Catharine lost him his place, and the Reformers lost a friend at court.

Then Sir Thomas More, another remarkable historical character, became Henry's chief minister, one of the most attractive and detestable, amiable and cruel, pious and bloodthirsty, saints that ever adorned the private life or disgraced the religious life of his times. He was one of those men of whom it may be said that but for their religion they would be the most estimable of men.

He killed Bainham for being a Protestant and the Protestants killed him for being a Catholic. But for the king he would probably have burned Latimer. Two years and a half, and his hour on the stage came to a bloody end.

The king appointed Latimer to a living at West Kingston, in Wiltshire, in 1531, and he retired from the court to the comparative seclusion of a rural parish, but there is no such thing as quiet or seclusion or silence for the bold and zealous Reformer. He preached at every opportunity and sought out opportunities to preach. He was "as sheep in the midst of wolves." The wolves were the bishops who thirsted for his blood because they winced under his preaching. They were reinforced by the country clergy, and Latimer was again in the hands of his enemies.

Among other counts in the indictment against him was that of preaching that there was no purgatory and no material fire in hell. He maintained that the fire could only be a figure, since you could not touch the soul with material fire.

This was especially displeasing to the persecutors, who would probably never have thought of fire as a punishment for heresy if they had not interpreted the Bible to mean that the Almighty had selected that kind of punishment for heretics. Those who chained the body of the heretic to the tree, and set fire to it, believed that the Deity was standing ready to cast his soul into equally literal flames and chains.

In 1532 he was summoned by the archbishop and bishops to answer to the charge

Hugh Latimer

of heresy, but Latimer was as wary before his accusers as he was bold in the pulpit. He answered discreetly. He observed that a curtain covered the fireplace, and that he was examined near this curtain. One of his examiners exclaimed: "I pray you, speak out, Master Latimer; I am very thick of hearing, and there be many that sit far off." This confirmed Latimer's suspicions, and he heard a pen taking down his answers behind the curtain.

He was required to subscribe to certain articles on pain of excommunication and death, and he did subscribe, whether to the full extent required is not known. The narrative here, as in several other parts, is obscure. That he made some kind of submission there is no doubt. He kneeled before the convocation and confessed that he had "misordered himself so far, in that he had so presumptuously and boldly preached, reproving certain things by which the people that were infirm hath taken occasion of ill."

He Weakens

He Weakens

In recalling the weakening of such men under such circumstances, remember their education, their times, the natural recoil from a death so horrible. Furthermore, Latimer was a feeble man physically; he was never free from bodily infirmities.

And that is not all. I cannot but infer from the tone and style of Latimer's preaching that he was something of what is now known as a Broad Churchman. It was difficult for him to put much more emphasis upon opposition to the dogmas than he did upon the dogmas themselves. He saw the fallacy and absurdity of transubstantiation, and baptismal regeneration, and the like, but he did not feel the necessity of sacrificing everything in doing away with them. He said: "Cannot we preach the gospel, and save men in spite of them? Shall we pull down the whole fabric to get rid of a few rotten timbers? At any rate there is no hurry. It is too soon to bring on a crisis."

An indication of this spirit is seen in the opinion he expressed with respect to a religious manual which he had, when a bishop, united with the other bishops in publishing: "It is a troublous thing to agree upon a doctrine in things of such controversy, every man, I trust, meaning well, and yet not all meaning one way." He hopes the king will tolerate the manual for a time, however uncertain it may sound. "He can separate for himself. So giving place for a season to the frailty and gross capacity of his subjects." What he advised the king to do he did himself. He bore with the "gross capacity" of his associates and opponents.

Being further molested he appealed to the king, and the king delivered him out of the hands of the Philistines. He returned to his parish and his preaching.

The tide turned again in favor of the Reformers. The archbishop of Canterbury and primate, Warham, died and Cranmer succeeded him and made Latimer a bishop.

Thus Cranmer became archbishop of Canterbury and primate of the English Church in 1533. Here is another historic character, another name of lustre and renown in the history of the Reformation, another martyr, one of the three martyrs whose martyrdom gave the Protestants their greatest impulse, Latimer, Ridley, and Cranmer.

Cranmer acquiesced in the burning of Frith for denying that the bread of the supper is Christ's body. You will find the very words for which Frith was burned at the close of the Communion service in the Church of England Book of Common Prayer: "The natural body and blood of our Saviour Christ are in heaven and not here, it being against the truth of Christ's natural body to be at one time in more places than one."

Cranmer tried to persuade Frith out of this heresy, and was himself persuaded of its truth by Frith's writings and was burned for adopting them. Like Forest and Bilney he recanted, but afterward recanted his recantation. He held his right hand in the fire at the stake, until it was consumed, as a punishment for writing the recantation.

This reminds us of the success of persecution. If men of so much nerve and faith, and so much responsibility for their cause, almost abandon it in this awful moment, what must be the recoil and horror of men of weaker spirit? If the leaders shrink, what must be the shrinking of the masses? If martyrdom is an example to inspirit the occasional spirit of high degree, it is a disastrous discouragement to the common run of ordinary minds.

Here again we have the blood and mettle and stuff and stamina that holds on and never lets go, and wins in the end, whether it be the reformation of a church, or the pushing of an idea, or the colonization of a continent. It is the Teutonic, Viking, Northern, Saxon, Anglo-Saxon, pertinacity which will die game if it must die.

Race Again

It carried Latimer to a high place. Through Cranmer's influence he was reappointed royal chaplain and was made Bishop of Worcester. Instead of the stake he had a seat on the episcopal bench. He

The Tide Turns

The Tide Turns

preached as boldly in the bishop's lawn as in the priest's gown.

His sermon at his consecration was another shell in the camp of his enemies. They denounced it as seditious and complained of it to the king, who summoned him to answer for it. He said: "If your grace will allow me for a preacher, give me leave to discharge my own conscience and to frame my doctrine according to my audience... I would be a dolt to preach at the borders of your realm as I preach before your grace."

This was one of the daring preacher's adroit answers. Henry was satisfied. His liking for Latimer saved him, and the wolves must leave their prey again. The stake was cheated of its victim once more. The time had not yet come.

In one of his sermons before the royal family and nobles he declaims against covetousness, and this is a specimen of his preaching: *Specimen of his Preaching*

"Take heed and beware of covetousness. Take heed and beware of covetousness. Great complaints there are of it and much crying out and preaching, but little amendment. Covetousness is the root of all evil. Then have at the root. Out with your swords, ye preachers, and have at the root. Stand not ticking and toying at the branches, for new branches will spring out again. . . . Strike at the root and fear not these men of power, these oppressors of the needy. Fear them not but strike at the root."

He denounced the whole hierarchy of ecclesiastics, bishops, abbots, priests—as strong thieves and jolly fellows with golden chains and velvet gowns.

He was appointed to preach the opening sermon before the Convocation in 1536. It was the highest assembly known to the church outside of Rome, and this was the highest place he was to fill until he should stand at the stake. St. Paul's Cathedral was crowded with ecclesiastics. The powerful Lord Cromwell, vicar general, presided.

Cranmer, who was to follow Latimer to the stake, sat in the primate's chair,

Honors Thicken

and others of the coming martyrs were present, and those who were to burn them. The great majority of that vast assembly thirsted for Latimer's blood while they listened to his sermon.

It was the hour of their discomfiture and his triumph. Now was his head high and lifted up above his enemies round about him, abbots, bishops, priests; they hated him with what Wesley calls "pious venom." He rose in the pulpit and exclaimed: "What fruit has come of your long and great assembly? What one thing that the people have been the better of a hair? These are our holy men that say they are dead to the world, and none are more lively to the world. God commands you to feed his sheep, and you feed yourselves from day to day wallowing in delight and idleness.

"Ye have not deceived God, but yourselves; his gifts and benefits shall be to your greater damnation. Because ye have despised the clemency of the Master ye have deserved the severity of the Judge.

"Let us see an account of your stewardship. God will visit you. He will come. He will not tarry long. In the day in which we do not look for him, he will come and cut you in pieces and give you your portion with the hypocrites, where there shall be wailing and gnashing of teeth."

At this convocation fourteen articles of faith were agreed upon, which made the first creed of the English Church. They were a compromise; some of them were designed to conciliate the Reformers, and some of them to conciliate their persecutors. They pleased neither party, and displeased both parties. Transubstantiation was retained to gratify Henry, who never abandoned it—he was saved if that could save him.

On the whole there was progress for the Protestants. Although the pope's authority was not entirely done away, it was hopelessly broken, and Tyndale's translation of the Bible was chained in every church, and any one might step in and read it.

1538

In 1538 came a cloud over the Reformer's good name and fame; we are astounded to find our great martyr joining in the martyrdom of another. Cranmer, who was himself to burn, concurred in the burning of Friar Forrest for refusing to acknowledge the supremacy of Henry over the pope. Cromwell appointed Latimer to preach upon the occasion.

We are astounded. We start back. Is this history? Yes, this is history, this is the history of the church of Jesus Christ, this is the history of the religion of peace to men.

Forrest's murder was more cruel and atrocious than that of any of them. He was put into an iron cage and the cage was surrounded by the fagots. The fagots were set on fire. While Forrest was slowly roasting alive in his iron cage, by command of the foremost Reformers and Protestants of that day, one of them, Hugh Latimer, preached.

It is a miserable spectacle this. We account for it by the hardening influence of a corrupt religion. None of the Reformers, inclusive of our own immediate ancestors, the Puritans, ever outgrew the vindictive cruelty of their religious education.

Henry and his tools passed what was known as "the bloody act of six articles, and the whip with six stings." By this act the denial of transubstantiation was made punishable with death, and the denial of other articles incurred fine and imprisonment. Then came a reaction.

Then came a Reaction

The Reformers rebelled. Latimer resigned his bishopric. He was tried for heresy and imprisoned in the Tower during the last years of Henry's reign, 1546.

Henry died and upon the accession of Edward VI. Latimer was set at liberty and his bishopric was offered him, but he declined it. He was probably wearied out with court life. He could do little or nothing to correct its morals or utilize it for the benefit of the new opinions. He

Edward VI. is King

Edward VI. is King

has a curious way of disappearing from the history of his times.

Latimer was an agitator, and was better at creating public opinion than utilizing it. He went everywhere preaching the word as he understood it, but now he would not preach long. Soon his voice was to be stifled in the flames.

The young king reigned only six years, then died, and with him died the hopes of the Reformers.

The curtain rose then upon one of the most pathetic tragedies of English history, the ten days' reign and the execution of Lady Jane Grey, although as innocent as any person now living.

Edward was succeeded by Mary I. The blood of two hundred and fifty men and fifty women is on her skirts. One hundred of them were starved and otherwise tortured. She did what she could to arrest the Reformation, and restore England to the authority of the pope.

Bloody Mary

So the tide turned again, and Latimer was again a prisoner in the Tower, along with Cranmer and Ridley. Here he endured hunger, cold, solitude, and every privation. In 1554 he was summoned to answer for his heresy at Oxford. The commissioners appointed to examine him with Cranmer and Ridley, simply came together to enjoy their triumph. They chuckled, for it was their turn now. The bishop who arraigned them from the pulpit of St. Paul's, was now arraigned by them. The sheep were in the clutches of the wolves at last.

No wisdom of serpents or harmlessness of doves could save them. Latimer's answers were received with jeers and laughter. He was feeble as well as old, and tortured with disease as well as bowed down with age. They taunted the old man.

Latimer was so faint that he begged that they would do their worst quickly. "What thou doest do quickly." He was thrown again into the common jail for a year, when he was again and for the last time brought before the inquisition of Bloody Mary.

Bloody Mary

He was feebler than before, for his imprisonment had told upon him, but although his body tottered his mind was firm.

The inquisitors twitted him with want of learning. He replied: "You look for learning in one who has bare walls for his library, without book, pen, or ink." He congratulated them on their goodly victory over such a man.

They could taunt him and defy him, but they could not break his spirit or destroy his faith. He was urged to recant, to declare for the pope and save his life. He refused with a spirited and noble scorn. He knew that if he should recant they would murder him all the same. It was the revenge of those who had been put in the wrong. They were condemned, Latimer and Ridley, and on the 16th of October, 1555, they were conducted to the stake. The monument to their memory is seen on the spot where they perished, at Oxford, England.

Latimer was bowed under his burthen of years, trials, and privations; the disorders that had always tortured him had been aggravated by age. The sun shone unobscured; it was a pleasant autumn day.

They came to the stake, and Ridley asked permission to say a word or two, whereupon the vice-chancellor ran and laid his hand over the martyr's mouth, and told him if he would recant he should have liberty not only to speak but to live. "All that a man hath will he give for his life," unless he has the sustaining power of the martyr's spirit. Ridley replied: "So long as the breath is in my body I will never deny my Christ, and his known truth. God's will be done in me. I commit our cause to Almighty God, who shall impartially judge all."

Latimer added, "There is nothing hid but shall be made manifest."

Ridley distributed his gown, watch, and other keepsakes among his friends.

Latimer wore a long shroud reaching over his feet under his threadbare coat. A New Testament hung to his girdle. His spectacles hung around his neck. He

Martyrdom

was stripped of these and his outer garments were removed. They take off his socks and his feet were shod with only the preparation of the gospel of peace. The bowed, withered, grayhaired old man rose erect in his shroud.

A murmur of sympathy mingled with horror, ran through the spectators. They were moved, and yet they were probably as familiar with the burning of a heretic as we are with elections as the permanent amusement of a free people.

An iron chain was fastened around Latimer and Ridley and fastened to the stake. A bag of gunpowder was tied to each of them by friends, an act of mercy. It was designed to hasten their end. So much escape of suffering was allowed them by the Holy Church of Bloody Mary.

Ridley asked a friend to look after some cases of charity, especially that of his poor sister. He said nothing was on his conscience except that. His last thoughts, even in these awful straits, were of others, and not of himself. They brought the fagots and laid them about the feet of the Reformers, whereupon Latimer exclaimed: "Be of good comfort, Master Ridley, and play the man. We shall this day light such a candle, by God's grace, in England, as I trust shall never be put out."

Everything was now ready. The fagots were set on fire. As the flames rose about them, Ridley cried: "Lord, unto thy hands I commend my spirit. Lord, Lord, receive my spirit."

Latimer held out his arms as if to embrace the flames and welcomed his last enemy. He prayed: "O Father in heaven, receive my soul."

He stroked his face with his hand as though washing his face with the fire, and defying it to touch his soul. The gunpowder exploded and Latimer died.

Ridley burned more slowly. The fire joined his enemies in taunting him. He cried, "Let the fire come; I cannot burn." He tried to get more into the flame. Some one mercifully assisted the flame to reach him. The gunpowder exploded at last and he likewise died.

Martyrdom

It was finished. They had played the man. They had kindled a light that should never be put out.

If we play the man, we shall see by the light of the fire of this stake how un-Christlike and execrable is this persecuting intolerance. Have we played the man and the Christian to that extent?

For the want of this manliness the German Protestants refused coalition with the Protestants of England. Melancthon called the English martyrs the "devil's martyrs." When the English Protestants fled to the continent, they were driven with abuse and insult from every port and town and hearthstone where the disciples of Luther prevailed. The enmity between Calvinists and Lutherans was as fierce as that between Reformers and Catholics. The Lutherans avowed that, "rather than tolerate such heretics as the Calvinists they would turn back to the Church of Rome."

A strange, strange, strange history is the history of the breaking away of England from the dominion of Rome. It was not until Elizabeth came to the throne in 1558 that the separation of the Church of England from the Church of Rome was consummated.

Parliament established the Reformed religion in 1559, four years after Latimer and Ridley had been burned for preaching it, and Elizabeth became supreme governor in spiritual and ecclesiastical as well as temporal things.

Then came the turn of the Protestants to persecute. They did not use the fire so freely, but they used fines, imprisonment, and torture as freely as they dared. They had no more idea of tolerating the Catholics than the Catholics had of tolerating them, and it was Protestant eat Protestant. The Reformed faith made it so hot for the Puritans in England that the Puritans fled to this country and made it hot for the Quakers.

Religion entered into the cause of the last war between Turkey and Russia. The crescent on one flag means one religion, the cross on the other flag means another religion—does it not? Both Russian Christians and Turkish Mohammedans were as mercilessly intolerant as were the good Christians of the time of Saint Henry VIII., "Defender of the Faith."

Did I not hear Protestant preachers during that war express the wish and the prayer from the pulpit that the Turks might be crushed out and destroyed from the face of the earth? Could any motive short of a religiously vindictive one prompt such a wish or inspire such a prayer?

Have you not known recent instances of members of a family being disowned and banished for becoming Catholics or Protestants? Nay, do not some have the door shut against them and the heart steeled against them for going from one Protestant denomination to another?

What is this but the spirit of persecution? What is this but the intolerance that has covered the history of our religion with reproach as with a garment and reddened every step of its progress with blood?

It certainly is. When we feel it moving

within us in the treatment of the parent, child, or friend, we may know we share in the religious malignity that burned Latimer at the stake. And we will never play the man nor act the Christian until the last symptom of this persecuting intolerance is eradicated from our hearts.

"By this shall all men know that ye are my disciples, if ye have love one to another."

www.ingramcontent.com/pod-product-compliance
Lightning Source LLC
Chambersburg PA
CBHW021818230426
43669CB00008B/796